A NEW VISION FOR THE CATHOLIC CHURCH

Gerry O'Hanlon SJ

A New Vision for the Catholic Church

A VIEW FROM IRELAND

the columba press

First published in 2011 by
the columba press
55A Spruce Avenue, Stillorgan Industrial Park,
Blackrock, Co Dublin

Cover by Bill Bolger
Origination by The Columba Press
Printed in Ireland by Brunswick Press Ltd, Dublin

ISBN 978 1 85607 729 3

Contents

'Where there is no vision, the people perish' (Proverbs 29:18)

Then Yahweh answered and said, 'Write the vision down, inscribe it on tablets, to be easily read, since this vision is for its own time only: eager for its own fulfilment, it does not deceive; if it comes slowly, wait, for come it will, without fail' (Habakkuk 2:2-3)

Foreword

This book originated in a series of evenings given by Fr Gerry O'Hanlon SJ in Manresa, the Jesuit Centre of Spirituality in Dublin. That series, like this book, focused on a crucial issue facing the Catholic Church in Ireland today: what is our vision for the church? For the past twenty years or so, the church in Ireland has seen a succession of scandals and institutional failures that have alienated further a generation of Irish people who were already feeling estranged from a structure they perceived as distant and irrelevant to their lives. Further shocking revelations from abroad – the US, Germany, Belgium and Australia among others – and the impenetrable nature of the church's institutions have only further fuelled the helplessness and anger felt by so many.

But the human heart continues to search. Many people in Ireland today are crying out for a glimmer of light, a sign of hope – a new vision. And the new vision, as it turns out, is also an old vision. Central to the teaching of Vatican II on the church is the ancient scriptural image of the People of God: the Israelite nation, battered and weary, being led by Moses through the desert on their way to the Promised Land. In our barren times, that image is perhaps even more appropriate than it was fifty years ago. Like them, we are discouraged. We are tired. We feel like giving up. We wonder where God is in all of this. We are tempted to turn to the false gods of our time. Where else can we turn?

In this book, Fr O'Hanlon is suggesting where to turn: to the inclusive vision and wisdom of Vatican II. St Paul tells us that 'there are many different gifts, but it is always the same Spirit,' and that 'the particular manifestation of the Spirit granted to each one is to be used for the general good' (1 Cor 12:4-7). We are one people, the People of God, with a great diversity of gifts. It is surely time for us to make use of all the gifts the Spirit gives the church in the service of the whole human family. With Jesus, the New Moses, as our Leader, we can find a way.

Paddy Carberry SJ
Director, Manresa

Introduction

The church is called to be 'the light of the nations' (*Lumen Gentium, Dogmatic Constitution on the Church*, Vatican II). Its mission is to preach the good news of the reign or kingdom of God, the reign of justice and peace which overcomes evil and sin. And so the church is called to be a sacrament or sign of intimate union with God, of the unity of all humankind (*LG*, 1), a sign of hope for the whole world that, often despite appearances, 'all will be well'. Each member of the church is called to holiness (*LG*, ch 5), to that unity of the two great commandments, love of God and love of neighbour.

The rhetoric is lofty, but the reality that we experience is different. Far from being a 'light for the nations' we often, today, experience the Catholic Church as a source of embarrassment and shame. The immediate cause of this is the awful reality of clerical child sexual abuse and the serious mishandling of this by church leaders. But, happy fault (*felix culpa*), through this awful reality more and more people are becoming aware of a wider and deeper malaise in our church, to do with a clericalist culture and overly centralised organisational structure that do scant justice to the nature of the church as the People of God (*LG*, ch 2)[1] and mean that the church is in need of more radical reform. This awareness is a grace and carries with it a responsibility: we are being asked by God, it seems to me, to re-examine what it means to be church, to imagine a new vision, and to begin to take the steps to implement this vision.

---

1. G. O'Hanlon, 'The Murphy Report – A Response', *The Furrow*, 61, February 2010, 82-91; 'The Future of the Catholic Church – a view from Ireland', *Studies*, 99, Autumn, 2010, 289-301; 'Culture and the Present Crisis in the Church', *The Furrow*, 61, December, 2010, 655-666

The situation is grave. An informal conversation has broken out among church members, including those who have 'left' the church, often out of the earshot of bishops and priests. This conversation is peppered with phrases like: 'They just don't get it'; 'Things will never change'; 'The bishops are the problem'; 'Rome is just as bad'; 'I am sick of the church'; 'It is not nice being a woman in this church'; 'Get real'; 'Nice documents are not enough'. The temptation to reject the institutional church is considerable and, in its place, to retreat into a privatised spirituality or, more rarely, a social activism inspired by gospel principles.

And yet, at times, we do catch a glimpse of the rich reality behind the lofty, even exhilarating rhetoric of church as 'light for the nations'. At baptisms, weddings, funerals, in the holy lives of individual women and men, in the gospel-inspired and church-affiliated work for justice and peace, we know that the church is being true to its vocation and that, without it, we would be the poorer. Without the church it is easy to imagine the gospel message degenerating into sectarian factionalism at worst, and, at best, a sincere spirituality which would simply not have the 'institutional legs' to survive the tough challenges thrown up by the message of Jesus to our world.

As a boy in Drumcondra in the late 50s I experienced a then traditional form of this ecclesial richness – I recall the excitement and pageantry of Corpus Christi processions, the Papal and national flags flying from my granny's house, the solemn procession with the Blessed Sacrament, incense, and hymn singing. All seemed well. We know now that all was not well then, and is not well now. The 'don't ask, don't tell' culture referred to in the Murphy Report has revealed a church with major institutional problems. These concern, in particular, the mode of governance and distribution of power at all levels, the absence of the voice and perspective of women in decision-making bodies, and the failure to consult adequately in forming church teaching and law. The latter means that, particularly in matters relating to sexuality and gender, the 'sense of the faithful' does not receive what is taught in peace, as rooted in their Christian experience of life. There has been revealed a culture of undue deference in our church and a lack of collective responsibility that extends much more deeply and widely than the issue of sexual abuse alone.

We know that, above all, it is God who will renew us and our church, that our holiness in our pilgrim way will be 'genuine though imperfect' (*LG*, 48), and that we will always remain a church of both saints and sinners. Still, this eschatological perspective is never a pretext to avoid repentance of those sins of which, through God's grace, we become aware. We are called, then, to play our indispensable role, imbued with the patient love of God, in the renewal of our church. We do so with some humility, aware that the high moral ground proved lethal for the Pharisees, Pelagius and so many other zealous historical reformers. But we do so as well with a firm commitment rooted in our hope of the guidance of the Holy Spirit at this time of challenge and opportunity, this *kairos* for our church.

In this context, despite the urgency and gravity of our situation, it would not be wise to respond in a simplistically reactionary way, substituting one kind of populist authoritarianism for another that was elitist. We need some careful thinking to inform what I believe is a period of 'communal discernment' for our church – here in Ireland, but universally also. In this context too it is a hopeful sign that the informal conversations referred to above are now also taking place more formally at parish and even diocesan level in the Catholic Church in Ireland.[2] At the nub of our problem is the need to find a better balance between centralisation, papal primacy and the proper autonomy of local churches and of the lay faithful in particular. In this context I like

---

2. 'It is clear that, this year, the church in Ireland has experienced the beginnings of structured dialogue at many levels' – Bishop Seamus Freeman, Ossory, in 'Rite and Reason', *The Irish Times*, Tuesday December 28, 2010, reporting as Chairman of the Bishops' Council for Pastoral Renewal and Faith Development on the fruits of responses to Pope Benedict's Pastoral Letter to the Catholics of Ireland from parishes and dioceses throughout the island of Ireland, including over 3000 written contributions.

the formulation of Ladislas Orsy: 'We are at a groundbreaking stage. For this reason we ought to formulate our questions with utmost care. Our aim is to search for better balances without damaging vital forces.'[3] We need, then, to be true to what is good in our identity and history, and yet to respond more adequately to the needs of the world of today.

Perhaps the recent (2010) Papal visit to Britain can be a good image of this need for better balance 'without damaging vital forces' – it was wonderful that the visit gave so much encouragement and put the issue of religion firmly back in the public square, and yet one wondered if such enormous focus on one person and his office could facilitate the need for local churches to exercise their divinely mandated autonomy without undue deference.[4]

I will be proposing that the Second Vatican Council – the most authoritative, modern faith and gospel-based vision of the church that we have at our disposal – is our best resource for the kind of renewal that we require (chapter three). In returning to this vision we will of course have to take into account developments that have occurred since the council, the new 'signs of the times' which have arisen since (chapters four and five). And, to understand Vatican II itself, we need first to look back, even very briefly, at where it all started (with Jesus Christ) and how we got to where we were when Vatican II was called into being by Pope John XXIII (chapters one and two). This 'looking back' is not primarily an exercise in history as such, but more a necessary context-setting through which we may better formulate our questions. In this way we can hope to note some of the complexity that is involved and yet do so in a way that does not paralyse, but allows us to be better prepared to discern and take responsibility for the concrete actions needed to shape the future that God wants and is leading us towards. I will propose that a National Assembly or Synod of the Irish Catholic Church would

3. L. Orsy, Receiving the Council, MN: Liturgical Press, 2009, p 12
4. See also Kevin T. Kelly, 'The Pope in Britain', The Furrow, 61, 2010, 609-612

be the best next step on our journey into this future (chapter five and Appendix). I want, then, to present a kind of rudimentary ecclesial faith-map, with a view to allowing us to imagine the direction we need to take, and the kind of reasonable detours and bridge-building we need to pursue in order to overcome our current road-blocks and return to the 'way of the Lord' that true discipleship involves.

This book originated in a number of talks given last October, 2010, as part of the Arrupe Seminar Series at Manresa Jesuit Centre of Spirituality, the majority of participants being lay faithful. I want to express my particular gratitude to those wonderfully engaged and constructively critical participants, to the pioneering Director of Manresa, Fr Paddy Carberry SJ, who invited me to speak and to staff member Cormac McConnell who brought the event to fruition with such energy and commitment. The book makes no pretensions to theological originality, except in so far as it aims to deepen a conversation between a contemporary, scholarly theology of church on the one hand, rooted in scripture, tradition and the Second Vatican Council, and, on the other, the 'signs of our times' here in Ireland, but also more universally in the Catholic Church. As such it may serve as a background resource to all those who are concerned about renewal of the Catholic Church in Ireland or further afield, be they Catholics, other Christians, those who are seekers and doubters of all kinds or, indeed, interested fellow citizens. It may be of relevance, then, to the general reader, while being of particular interest to those with even a little theological background. I would hope, too, that the book may stimulate theologians to widen and deepen a conversation which will become more and more necessary as attempts at renewal gather pace.

I would also like to thank my Jesuit Provincial John Dardis, and his successor Tom Layden, for their support, not least in relieving me of the duties of administration to enable this project to be realised; to the then Acting Director of the Jesuit Centre for Faith and Justice, Eoin Carroll, and his successor John Guiney, SJ, as well as all the staff of the Centre, in particular Cathy

Molloy (who read and annotated a first draft of this text) for all their support; to Pat Coyle of the Jresuit Communications Centre; to fellow members of the Council of Justice and Peace of the Irish Episcopal Conference, with whom I am engaged on a similar project; to Seán O Boyle and The Columba Press for their unfailing courtesy and professionalism; and to my family Eileen and Randal, Frank and Freddy, and friends, in particular Fiona Fullam, Brian Lennon, Bill Toner and Jim Corkery for all their unfailing encouragement and challenge. To one and all I am grateful, beyond words.

CHAPTER ONE

Historical Context:
New Testament and up to 19th century

In this very brief historical survey our focus will be strictly on ecclesiology and, within this, even more sharply on the kind of institutional structure and culture which is consistent with the message of Jesus and with the normative development of this message through the centuries. Moreover, the survey is undertaken precisely to illuminate our current situation and so need not attend to all other aspects of this historical legacy.

1.1 New Testament (see R. McBrien, *The Church*, Part Two, 23-59)[1] Jesus came to preach the good news of the kingdom of God. The church is the sign and instrument of this kingdom in history (*LG*, 1) – one notes, from the start, the notion of the church as being in service of a greater reality and not simply identified with it.

Even if Jesus did not explicitly found the church in the sense of formally setting up a new organisation with a blueprint for its structures, he did lay the foundations for the church in various ways. So, for example, there was the gathering of disciples, the sending out to proclaim the good news, the provision for continuity in the injunction to 'do this in remembrance' of me that was spoken at the real and symbolic meal that was the Last Supper and is the Eucharist of today, and the promise of the presence of the Holy Spirit (especially as recounted at Pentecost). There was, in addition, the distinct identity of the Twelve (recalling the twelve tribes of Israel) and a certain pre-eminence of Peter within the group of twelve (the famous Mt 16:18 text so central

1. References are to Richard P. McBrien, *The Church*, New York: Harper Collins, 2009 (original 2008)

to Catholic ecclesiology – 'on this rock I will built my church'), with the charge to Simon Peter to 'strengthen your brothers' (Lk 22: 31-34). Within all this the Second Vatican Council in its decree on the laity (*Apostolicam Actuositatem*) notes the 'proper and indispensable role in the mission of the church' of the laity (*AA*, 1), quoting scriptural texts such as Acts 11:19-21; 18:26; Romans 16:1-16; Philippians 4:3. Ladislas Orsy (45) notes that 1 Corinthians is addressed not to any leader but to the church at Corinth 'called to be saints' (1 Cor 1:2), in which there is a multitude of gifts and charisms – for example, healings, miracles, prophecy, discernment, tongues, interpretation, bringing order to meetings but not extinguishing the Spirit (1 Cor 12:7-8 ,Orsy 45).

But if this much is relatively uncontroversial, I note that we ought not to be too prescriptive about what we can derive as normative for present church structures from the New Testament. So, for example, Michael Fahey,[2] drawing on the work of Raymond Brown, notes the diversity of churches and structures that existed in early Christianity, associated with particular scriptural inspiration (344-347). He indentifies over 10 such different church types and structures, modelled after the likes of Matthew, Paul, John and so on, and with both women and men playing prominent and diverse roles. This diversity among churches also derives from their association with particular geographic locations (like Rome, Ephesus, Jerusalem, Antioch). In particular, while a certain pre-eminence of Peter is established, nonetheless it is James who is leader of the most important early church at Jerusalem and who presides at the ground-breaking Council of Jerusalem (to do with the treatment of non-Jews, Gentiles), while Paul, for one, felt free to confront Peter when he judged that he was wrong (Gal 2:11). Indeed in Acts 1-12, where Peter's leadership is most clearly portrayed, decisions are also made by 'the Twelve' or 'the apostles' or 'the church', and not only by Peter. It is, for example, 'the Twelve' who decide to ap-

---

2. M. Fahey, 'Church', in Francis Schüssler Fiorenza and John P. Galvin, eds, *Systematic Theology*, Dublin: Gill and Macmillan, 1992, 327-398.

point seven men to serve in the role of what we would later call deacons (Acts 6:1-7). Nor are 'the Twelve' the sole participants in Jesus' authority – there are also prophets, teachers, evangelists, presbyters and others (1 Cor 12:28; Eph 4:11 – McBrien, 287). Women played a prominent role in the churches at Corinth, Philippi, and Rome, performing some of the same functions and displaying some of the same gifts as men (McBrien, 43). None of Paul's letters say anything about who presided at the eucharistic meals, while Raymond Brown reminds us that the owners of some of the house churches at this time were women (McBrien, 43).

What emerges from the New Testament is that the office or ministry of leadership is always for service, that it can take different forms (even episcopacy, as opposed to leadership by elders, is not universally established until the mid-second century – McBrien, 44), and that while the chief ministry of the universal church is Petrine, nonetheless it is quite clear that Peter's authority was neither absolute nor monarchical. Ecclesiologically it was the case that each local church is the church in that particular place, while the church is the communion (*koinonia* – 1 Jn 1:3) of all the local churches which together constitute the one universal church (McBrien, 28-9). Over time a greater uniformity did develop, both for good reasons (the need for stability and accord as number and locations grew) and for bad (over-identification with secular models of leadership from the Roman Empire on).

This brief overview indicates that, while there is certain minimal normative content to the New Testament teaching on church, still there is no uniform structural organisation recommended, and local churches felt free to develop their own style in response to particular situations and pastoral needs (McBrien, 57-8). In particular there was a dynamic interplay between what we would now call collegial and primatial elements of authority.

The key question for us, it seems to me, is to try to determine how this balance between the collegial and primatial elements at all levels, that is apparent in the New Testament, is best lived out in our day, given our understanding that the guidance of the

Holy Spirit has been part of this development over the centuries, and given our own particular situation and pastoral needs.

1.2 Up to 19th century (McBrien, Part III, 61-90)

It will be sufficient for our purposes to simply note once again some of the main developments that have particular relevance to our theme.

The Edict of Milan (313)

The Edict of Milan of the Emperor Constantine ushered in an era of church-state concord, after the persecutions of the first few centuries, in which religion was afforded the protection of the state, as well as favours and privileges: 'The clergy became, in effect, civil servants with all of the advantages, financial and otherwise, attached thereto' (McBrien, 66). Titles, honours, dress – they all date from around this period. And as the centuries went on there were more or less close ties, to the point of almost identification at times, between church and state – Charlemagne being crowned by the Pope, Papal armies and states, the religious wars, the monasteries as the bulwark of a disordered society. We are familiar, since Vatican II, with the notion of church-state separation, non-confessional states – this was far from the Catholic understanding right up to the 19th century and beyond.

The question that emerges from this whole development is to what extent purely secular and civil forms of government and power, with their tendencies towards centralisation and coercion, over-influenced the more collegial ministry of leadership as service revealed by God in the person of Jesus Christ?

The Gregorian Reform

Pope Gregory VII (1073-1085) tackled clerical corruption, simony, nepotism and lay investiture (the interference of temporal rulers in the internal life of the church, especially with regard to the appointment and installation of bishops and abbots). I simply note that here, as elsewhere historically, we have indications of lay involvement in episcopal appointments which, because human, was open to distortion. This does not of course mean that there should be no lay involvement in the future appointment of bishops – but it does counsel us to avoid any simplistic recourse to lay involvement without the kind of thinking through of the nature of this involvement which would reduce the risk of repeating past mistakes. This was also around the time of the East-West schism (1054): there was a felt need, it would seem, for a stronger central ecclesial authority in the West. Gregory met this need, helping to free the church from political domination too, in the form of the German Emperor Henry IV. In doing so, the role and power of the papacy was stressed to an unprecedented degree – the pope came to be seen as the supreme judge of all, including the bishops and abbots, with unlimited powers of absolution and excommunication and the right to depose Emperors.

In earlier centuries the title 'pope', which means father, was applied to every bishop in the West, while in the East it seems to have been used of priests as well as a special title of the Patriarch of Antioch. In 1073, however, Pope Gregory VII formally prohibited the use of the title of all except the Bishop of Rome (Mc Brien, 93). Similarly, in the first millennium, popes functioned largely as mediators – they did not claim for themselves the title 'Vicar of Christ' (the most traditional title accorded the pope, but only from the end of the fourth century, is that of Vicar of Peter – McBrien, 107), they did not appoint bishops,[3] they did not govern the universal church through the Roman Curia, they did not even convene Ecumenical Councils as a rule (McBrien, 100). Out of Gregory's reform grew the discipline of canon law and, in the 12th century, the first attempt at universal law, Gratian's *Decretum* (1140) which was standard until the then new Code of 1917.

It should be noted that this emphasis on centralisation and

---

3. As one example among many, the weekday Missal (London: HarperCollins, 1982) notes in introduction to the December 7th feast-day of St Ambrose of Milan that '... while still a catechumen, he was elected Bishop of Milan by the laity – he hesitated to accept, but was baptised and ordained ...'

the role of the papacy was new: in earlier centuries the primacy of the Petrine office was understood very much along the lines of 'first among equals' (*primus inter pares*), a court of last appeal, a service of unity and love, and even ecumenical councils had little direct papal involvement, albeit confirmation of their decisions by the pope was important. All through this era there was great autonomy of local churches, local councils and synods were frequent, the different Metropolitans and Patriarchies balanced the power of Rome. And so, for example, Fahey (349), speaking about the second and third centuries, notes that 'What needs to be explained about the early church is not how a local, city-based church came to see itself as autonomous, but rather how a local church came to choose various modalities for wider fellowship. For mainline Christian churches, being autonomous never meant sterile isolation.' The default position, in other words, was autonomy in communion.

Again, the question is to what extent is this centralisation appropriate for our needs today, and to what extent are we free to adjust what was developed historically along these lines?

The Great (Western) Schism (1378-1417)

The Great Western Schism meant that for over forty years there were at least two claimants to the Chair of Peter – interesting that the church survived for over forty years even when there was sharp disagreement about who was the legitimate pope! The remarks of McBrien are pertinent: 'The principal historical elements of the Great Schism challenge an ecclesiological assumption that was common from Vatican I to Vatican II, namely, that, in the end, the pope alone determines the nature and moral demands of the Catholic faith and that, without a pope, the church can only drift in a rudderless, circular fashion. The ecclesiological foundations for both assumptions was laid down, in large part, during the pontificate of Gregory VII in the late eleventh century and remained normative for many Catholics throughout the second millennium, reaching its initial apex in the pontificate of Innocent III (1198-1216) and Boniface

VIII (1295-1303) and then being reconstituted in a more sophistic-
ated and nonimperial form in the lengthy pontificate of John
Paul II (1978-2005)' (McBrien, 78).[4]

The Schism was brought to an end by the Council of
Constance (1414-1418), but in doing so it created the movement
known as conciliarism which effectively put a general council of
the church above the pope – after all, this council was not convened by a pope, it deposed two claimants to the role, secured
the voluntary abdication of a third, and elected a new pope ac-
ceptable to all. This council, in which there were non-episcopal,
even lay, delegates with rights of full participation, also mandated that future general councils meet at regular intervals.

In succeeding centuries many raised questions about the
legitimacy of Constance and, in any case, there was a return to
the papal-juridical mode of ecclesiology especially in the context
of the Reformation: but one can see that the question raised by
Constance, and rooted in the practice of the early church and
sacred scripture, was precisely the question that Vatican II was
to return to in its retrieval of the doctrine of collegiality as a way
of balancing that of papal primacy.

The Reformation
One of the ecclesiological causes of the Reformation was the corruption of the Renaissance papacy, marked by nepotism, simony,
military expeditions, financial manipulation, political intrigue,
and even murder (McBrien, 80). This was a papacy already
weakened by the Great Western Schism and now challenged in
its imperial self-understanding by the rise of national states. The
operative ecclesiology of the time had a hierarchical and institutional focus that was ill-suited to confront the new challenges
from the Reformers and from secular powers. In particular
papal resistance to legitimate calls for reform in the early six-
teenth century and the blatant failures of Lateran Council V

---

4. See also James Corkery, 'John Paul II: universal pastor in a global
age', James Corkery and Thomas Worcester, eds, *The Papacy since 1500*,
Cambridge University Press, 2010, 223-242, especially 238-242

(1512-17) in this respect represent a grievous miscalculation of the part of leadership (McBrien, 80).

In this context one way of understanding the Reformation is to see it as a rejection of the church's role of mediation, with stress now on the direct relationship between the individual believer and God, due not a little to the corrupt state of the church at the time. Because the Reformers tended to emphasis the 'invisible church', Catholic ecclesiologists reacted by stressing that the church was a visible, hierarchical, juridical society, a view which dominated Catholic ecclesiology for many centuries (McBrien, 80-81)

The French Revolution

The French Revolution, among other things, crushed Gallicanism (a highly nationalistic and anti-papal movement within the French Church – the German version, also in the 18th century, was known as Febronianism), but in doing so and with such anti-clerical violence it succeeded in making the French clergy more dependent on Rome. In this way it unwittingly fed the new spirit of ultramontanism – looking literally 'beyond the mountains', the Alps, to Rome – which was to have such an important role in Vatican I. Furthermore the hostility to religion and violence against clergy reinforced anti-democratic sentiment already prevalent in Catholic Church circles, due not least to the anti-Catholic rise of democracy in England.[5] The Revolution also led to a reinforcement of an Integralism that sought the ideal state as the confessional Catholic one. It was only in the *Decree on Religious Freedom* in Vatican II that the church definitively embraced democracy and the notion of church-state distinction as being positive.

Summary

This brief historical survey has given some flavour of the tension and balance between collegial and primatial elements de-

---

5. Cf Edmund Grace SJ, 'Democracy, Catholicism and the vice of "faction",' *Studies*, 99, Autumn, 2010, 323-332

veloped over many centuries. The observations of Ladislas Orsy with regard to a possible reform in the exercise of primacy are interesting: 'In truth, the possible extent and the scope of such a reform are largely unexplored. For a long time, hostile attacks on the papacy compelled Catholic scholars to defend it; they had little time and energy to analyse the inner structures and the workings of the primacy and then suggest reforms. The last significant work on this topic may have been the letter of St Bernard of Clairvaux ... (composed in 1150-2), to Pope Eugene III (reigned 1145-1153) in which the saint called on the pope to decentralise his government' (Orsy, 12). The full force of Orsy's words will become apparent in our presentation of the 19th century, the First Vatican Council and the period up to Vatican II.

CHAPTER TWO

Historical Context:
The Long Nineteenth Century, including
the First Vatican Council (1789-1958)

(McBrien, Parts III and IV, 85-149; O'Malley, Chapter Two, 53-92[1])

2.1 The Nineteenth Century

In his study on the Second Vatican Council John O'Malley refers to the 'long nineteenth century' for the Catholic Church as cov-ering a period from after the French Revolution to effectively 1958. He does so to convey a sense of the culmination of a centralising, monarchical form of ecclesiology, epitomised in the declaration in Vatican I of papal primacy and infallibility, and a predominantly negative attitude to developments in the secular sphere.

This ecclesiology grew in reaction to various cultural and historical developments which the church found to be inimical. We have already mentioned the Reformation and the French Revolution. Together with the Enlightenment, capitalism and the Industrial Revolution, the rise of democracy, these formed a cluster known as Modernism, also as Liberalism, in which the rights and freedom of the individual were newly discovered. In this new context the authority of reason was valued over the authority of tradition, of monarchs, of the church, and equality was preferred to hierarchy. It was in this period too that the papal states became under threat, symbolised by the seizing of Rome by the forces of the *Risorgimento* in 1870 and the consequent curtailment of the First Vatican Council. The church, apparently flourishing internally, turned away from engagement with the wider world except in terms of defiant opposition and developed the kind of siege mentality (Pius IX as 'prisoner of the Vatican') which was only lifted by John XXIII and the

---

1. The reference is to John O'Malley, *What Happened at Vatican II*, Massachusetts: Harvard University Press, 2008

Second Vatican Council. A rare exception to this policy of defiant opposition was the emergence of Catholic Social Teaching with Leo XIII (*Rerum Novarum*, 1891). Politically the 'Roman Question' was only solved in 1929 with the creation of the Vatican City as a sovereign state and the papacy's surrender of claims to Rome.

In an interesting comment on this period, Richard McBrien notes that 'from the time of the French Revolution ... until 1944, the popes held that a Catholic monarchy that gave legal recognition to the Catholic Church alone was the ideal form of government' (108) – it was only in 1944, after Rome had been liberated from German forces, that Pius XII explicitly recognised the positive value of democracy, thereby marking a break from an older tradition (108).

In this context of cultural wars between Liberalism/ Modernity and the Catholic Church the popes became teachers in a newly professed and more expanded way. The first papal encyclical was in 1740: in the 19th century it developed into the new genre that we are familiar with today. And gradually what the popes said in these encyclicals began to assume an irreversible quality, especially after the definition of infallibility (one is reminded of the phrase 'creeping infallibility' attributed to Yves Congar, describing the situation in the 20th century). O'Malley's comment on all this is interesting: 'As a consequence, Catholics increasingly looked to "Rome" not only as a court of final appeal but for answers to all questions' (56).

These answers came not only from the Pope himself but also from decrees of various congregations of the Curia, especially the Holy Office. And so it was in this era that the *Magisterium* increasingly came to mean not so much the teaching authority of the church, as specifically the teaching authority of the popes and their congregations (O'Malley, 57). This long nineteenth century represented the almost unmitigated triumph of ultramontanism, the concentration of authority in the papacy, and this was reflected not only theologically but also at the level of the corporate consciousness that reached down to the ordinary

Catholic in the pews – 'For the first time in history, thanks to the modern media, Catholics knew the name of the reigning pope and could recognise his face' (O'Malley, 57).

In this centralised but embattled context the popes defended by force their papal states and attacked what they saw as the errors of the day in their teachings. So, for example, Gregory XVI (1832) dismissed the idea that the church needed reform and attacked the notions of freedom of conscience and freedom of the press, while he inculcated obedience to princes. The major example of such teaching is the *Syllabus of Errors* of Pius IX (1864), condemning 80 errors, among them the idea that in 'our times' it was no longer proper or expedient for Catholicism to be the established religion of the state, with all others banned, and which concluded with the rejection of the notion that 'The Roman Pontiff can and should reconcile himself and make peace with progress, with Liberalism and with modern culture' (O'Malley, 60). A rejection of a Catholic form of Modernism (Tyrrell and others) was repeated, after Vatican I, by Pius XI in 1907 (in the encyclical *Pascendi*), accompanied by a document from the Holy Office (*Lamentabili*) condemning 65 propositions, followed by the Oath against Modernism in 1910 which was imposed on various office-holders in the church.

2.2 The First Vatican Council – 1870

The centralisation begun by Gregory VII in the 11th century, and reinforced by the context just described in the 19th century, reached its apotheosis in Vatican I. The two doctrines which are of interest to us are those contained in *Pastor Aeternus* – viz papal primacy and papal infallibility.

The doctrine of papal primacy was argued for as being consistent with the gradual emergence of Rome as an ecclesiastical court of last resort in the early centuries (99, McBrien). The decisive role of Leo I prior to the Council of Chalcedon (451) added to papal prestige. But it was after the East-West Schism and during the reign of Gregory VII, as we have seen, that the Bishop of Rome came to regard himself, and increasingly be regarded, as the universal primate of a universal church. In the eyes of the East this meant that 'the pastoral autonomy of the local churches and their bishops is all but lost' (McBrien, 99) – it is as if the pope is the bishop of every local church and the local bishops were simply his vicars or delegates. The Council of Lyons, 1274, claimed for the Roman church 'the supreme and full primacy and authority over the universal Catholic Church' (Mc Brien, 99-100) – it was on foundations like this that Vatican I made its declaration.

There was a good deal of ferment in the church prior to Vatican I's opening in 1869, Blessed Cardinal Henry Newman being one of those who opposed the strong forces arguing for the definition of papal infallibility and the type of ultramontanism which lay behind the monarchist claims for the exercise of papal primacy. Newman considered an ecumenical council the proper and usual setting for the exercise of papal infallibility and saw no need for the definition, especially if, as some of the ultramontanes wished, it would apply to virtually all papal pronouncements.[2]

Pastor Aeternus, promulgated in 1870, was meant to be a document on the church in general, but due to the untimely suspension of the council only the issues of primacy and infallibility were treated. The decree was passed in July 1870, a day before the outbreak of the Franco-Prussian War and the removal of French troops, protecting the pope, from Rome. The army of Victor Emmanuel took over Rome in September, in October a plebiscite approved the incorporation of Rome into the new Italian state, and in October Pius adjourned the council indefinitely. Its work, especially on the relationship between the papacy and the episcopate, would in some sense be completed at the Second Vatican Council almost 100 years later.

Of the two teachings of Vatican I that concern us, papal primacy is, arguably, the most important. I quote from the concluding formula:

2. Dermot Mansfield SJ, *Heart Speaks to Heart, The Story of Blessed John Henry Newman*, Dublin: Veritas, 2010, 157

So, then, if anyone says that the Roman pontiff has merely an office of supervision and guidance, and not the full and supreme power of jurisdiction over the whole church, and this not only in matters of faith and morals, but also in those which concern the discipline and government of the church dispersed throughout the whole world; or that he has only the principal part, but not the absolute fullness, of this supreme power; or that this power of his is not ordinary and immediate both over all and each of the churches and over all and each of the pastors and faithful: let him be anathema. (McBrien, 113-4).

How does one interpret this rather stark sounding formula? The German Chancellor Bismarck, engaged in his own cultural war against the Catholic Church, took what might seem to be the obvious meaning (1872) and declared that the council's definition had made the bishops nothing more than tools *(Werkzeuge)* of the pope, who now had more power than any absolute monarch of the past (O'Malley, 67). The German bishops answered him in a joint statement in early 1875, in which they insisted that the church could not be compared to an earthly kingdom nor the pope to an earthly king, that the bishops' authority was not in any way diminished by the decree on papal primacy, and that papal infallibility extended only to what scripture and tradition taught; they maintained, in short, that the definitions had changed nothing, 'not the least thing' (O'Malley, 67). In his treatment of the same statement, McBrien (114-115) notes that the German bishops declared that bishops have rights and duties given by divine ordinance that 'the pope has neither the right nor the power' to change and so it is not true that the 'bishops are now no more than tools of the pope, his officials, without responsibility of their own'. Later in 1875 the pope gave his solemn approval to this statement of the German bishops (McBrien, 115).

Indeed the text of *Pastor Aeternus* itself had also affirmed that 'this power of the supreme pontiff is far from obstructing the ordinary and immediate power of episcopal jurisdiction by

which individual bishops, placed by the Holy Spirit and successors of the apostles, feed and rule as true shepherds the individual flocks assigned to them' (DS 3061 – Fahey, 378-9), and goes
on to say that the pope is the tribunal of last appeal for the faithful (DS 3063 – Fahey 379). Fahey notes that the Pope's 'power' in
this context refers to his rightful authority and not to his right to
impose his will on others by force or intimidation; that 'ordinary' does not imply habitual, day-to-day use but that it belongs
to his office, is not delegated; and that 'immediate' refers to the
ability of faithful to appeal to him, not to direct governance on a
habitual basis (Fahey, 377-382). But Fahey notes too that it is regrettable that Vatican I did not indicate the limitations to papal
primacy in a clearer way and that Vatican II, while it balanced
papal prerogatives with a fuller consideration of the episcopacy,
often repeated much of the language and statements of Vatican I
without adequate nuancing and without sufficient reformul-
ation to resolve vexatious issues.

The teaching, then, is clearly affirming that papal primacy is
one not only of 'honour' but also of jurisdiction. And it seems
clear, not least from the felt need in Vatican II to debate the
issue, that as lived operatively within the Catholic Church since
Vatican I – but, as will be outlined later, since Vatican II also –
that, despite the reassurances of the German bishops and the in-
built nuances of the text itself, there has been a centralist,
monarchical, autocratic working out of this doctrine, accompanied indeed by the famous 'creeping infallibility' of Congar.

With regard to infallibility itself, it is clear that the infallibility,
in some sense, of the whole church had been a belief from earli-
est times, and the infallibility of councils which expressed universal teaching with subsequent papal approval was already a
conviction in the first millennium.[3] However, now the issue focused on the pope when engaged in some sense independently
in the act of teaching. Maximalist positions were rejected at

---

3. See Christopher O'Donnell O Carm, *Ecclesia, A Theological
Encyclopedia of the Church*, Minnesota: Liturgical Press, 1996, 212-217
under *Infallibility*.

Vatican I (that all papal teachings were infallible) and a highly conditional affirmation of papal infallibility was defined – the pope needs to be speaking *ex cathedra*, on matters of faith or morals, and in so doing he enjoys that infallibility which 'the divine Redeemer willed his church to enjoy', and, in these circumstances, his definitions are 'of themselves, and not by the consent of the faithful, irreformable' (McBrien, 117).

In fact theological opinion – and the practice of popes themselves – make it very clear that the exercise of this charism does involve a careful listening to the faith of the church, that an ecumenical council is the more appropriate forum for teaching of this kind and that this defined charism of papal infallibility is, for all practical purposes, 'unusable because of the careful restrictions placed upon it' (McBrien, 118). But of course expectations had been raised and they fed into the operative life of the church – and so, despite the very different tone of Vatican II, many Catholics since Vatican I have assumed that every papal pronouncement was to be regarded 'as if' it were infallible – a position unwittingly close to that of the extreme infallibilists of Vatican I. Newman, again, is instructive in this context. He was relieved that the definition adopted in Vatican I was couched in such relatively moderate terms, even if he understood that it leant itself to more extreme interpretations. He tried to reassure those among his worried contemporaries that in time what was now unbalanced would be put to right: 'Let us be patient, let us have faith, and a new pope, and a re-assembled council may trim the boat' (Mansfield, 164).

An amusing illustration of the enduring force of this exaggerated interpretation of papal infallibility is found in the autobiography of Archbishop Rembert Weakland of Milwaukee.[4] Weakland, from a family which suffered greatly from the poverty of the Great Depression, succeeded in obtaining a papal audience in 1970 with Paul VI for his mother and sister Betty when he himself was abbot primate of the Benedictine Order and be-

---

4. Rembert G. Weakland OSB, *A Pilgrim in a Pilgrim Church*, Michigan/Cambridge, UK: William B. Eerdmans, 2009

fore he became a bishop. The pope was very gracious. He received them in a small and intimate reception room with just a couch and a few comfortable chairs. He sat on the couch with Weakland's mother, took her hands in his and spoke to her in halting Italianised English. 'Mrs Weakland, your son good boy; does good things for the Benedictine Order', and so on. 'At the end he gave Mom a rosary he had just blessed. It became her prized object for years. As we left this little reception room and were walking down the gallery towards the elevator, I said slyly to her, 'Don't forget, Mom, he is infallible'. 'Yes, I know', she replied. 'That was the first faith crisis of my life' (Weakland, 222-223).

Both doctrines were highly controversial, resulting in some delegates leaving the council before voting and the formation in Germany of the Old Catholic Church. The distinguished German theologian Hermann Pottmeyer describes the tone and content of *Pastor Aeternus* as one-sided: 'As the minority (in opposition) anticipated, this document has proved harmful to the church. It was also unnecessary because the supreme pastoral authority of the papacy was not contested at the time. Nevertheless, the minority did prevent the acceptance of the extreme definition of papal infallibility, and eventually the views of the minority were confirmed by Vatican II' (McBrien, 118).

2.3 Post Vatican I developments

In the period between Vatican I and Vatican II there was, as might have been expected, a trend to consolidate the centralising dynamic in the church and the power of the papacy in particular. But there were also other, at first muted, trends which would lead to the new approach adopted in Vatican II.

Even if Leo XIII was conservative in many ways, he made a highly significant opening to the modern world with the first social encyclical *Rerum Novarum*. And while he continued to uphold the condemnation of any separation of church and state, still he allowed the legitimacy of the term 'Christian Democracy', while insisting on a conservative definition of it.

Pius X launched the project for the codification of Canon Law, completed after his death in 1917: this Code augmented papal authority, as, for example, in Canon 222 giving the pope control over councils and Canon 329 affirming that the pope appointed bishops in the church – thus marking the definitive abandonment of the free election of bishops for which the popes had at times fought so bitterly (O'Malley, 65). In his attack on Modernism within the church (1907–*Pascendi*) Pius refers to 'that most pernicious doctrine that would make of the laity a factor of progress in the church' and condemns Modernist positions which would hold that 'ecclesiastical government requires reformation in all its branches ... (that) a share in ecclesiastical government should therefore be given to the lower ranks of the clergy and even to the laity, and authority should be decentralised ... (that) the Roman Congregations, especially the Congregations of the Index and the Holy Office, are to be reformed' (O'Malley, 69-70). The year before (1906), in an encyclical to the French church, the same pope reiterated the hierarchical structure of the church, 'a society comprising two categories of persons, the pastors and the flock' – the duty of the former, which holds all authority in the church, is to direct the 'multitude', and it follows that 'the one duty of the multitude is to allow themselves to be led and, like a docile flock, to follow its pastors' (O'Malley, 65). This kind of formulation is extreme to modern sensibilities and yet it is instructive to note that it represented the dominant and operative theology of the time.

Later, in 1950, in his encyclical *Humani Generis*, Pius XII, albeit in more measured fashion, condemned the kind of 'novelties' that threatened to undermine Catholic truth and were resonant of the abuses of Modernism.

But other trends, subversive of this dominant orthodoxy, began to appear, at first under the umbrella title of Modernism, but then, understandably, after its condemnation, assuming other descriptions. These began to influence the church and even become part of official church teaching. These trends in-

cluded: a new approach to biblical studies;[5] a liturgical movement with strong historical roots which relativised current
practice and called for change; a neo-Thomism, inspired by Leo
XIII's prescription of Thomas Aquinas as the philosopher for
Catholic seminaries, leading, over time, to the engagement with
Modernity of scholars like Gilson and Maritain; the *nouvelle
théologie* of the likes of De Lubac, Daniélou, Chenu, Congar and,
later, others including von Balthasar and Ratzinger, inspired by
a return beyond the medieval to the patristic era, with some surprising results which also fed into Vatican II; the transcendental
Thomism of Maréchal, a retrieval of Aquinas in the context of
Immanuel Kant, leading to the likes of Rahner and Lonergan;
the return to Newman, with his notion of the development of
doctrine; the writings of John Courtney Murray on church-state
relations, at a time when citizens of the United States were tus-
sling with the issue of whether a Catholic could really be a suit-
able candidate for the Presidency (John Kennedy); the encyclical
Mystici Corporis of Pius XII in 1943, which, while it described the
relationship between head and members of the church in the hierarchical and juridical terms that had become traditional in the
second millennium, still it also insisted on the role of the Holy
Spirit in the church and thus on the balance that needed to be
struck between the hierarchical structures and the charismatic
gifts of the Holy Spirit (O'Malley, 85); and the encyclical
Mediator Dei (1947) of the same pope which effectively gave his
blessing to the Liturgical Movement, including the need for reform and change (O'Malley, 85-86).

Of course many of these trends and persons were opposed
by church authorities and even denounced and silenced for a
time: but gradually their influence gained ground and their
positions were largely vindicated at the Second Vatican Council.

---

5. In 1893 Leo XIII in *Providentissimus Deus* commended the old methods and never once encouraged the reading of the Bible by laity, but in
1902 he set up the Pontifical Biblical Commission and by 1943 Pius XII,
Divino Afflante Spiritu, gave approval to the new, historical methods of
biblical exegesis and scholarship first pioneered among Protestant
scholars.

2.4 Reflections on the Long Nineteenth Century

There are two underlying issues which characterise the tension between the more centralising, static and monarchical model emanating from the First Vatican Council and the other trends – often more in tune with the Modernity of secular culture – which tended to challenge the *status quo*.

First there was that move from what Lonergan calls a classically minded consciousness in which stability and the *status quo* were treasured and assumed to be normative because this is the way things had always been, to an historically minded consciousness in which it was realised that considerable change had in fact occurred down through the years and that 'if it was not always thus, it need not always be thus' (O'Malley, 77). Lonergan observes succinctly: 'What ended classicist assumptions was critical history.'[6] And so, for example, in 1955 Brian Tierney published *Foundations of the Conciliar Theory* in which he showed that in the Middle Ages reputable canonists assumed that the responsibility for the good of the church was distributed among various offices and corporations, each of which had its own intrinsic (not delegated) authority, that the episcopal office reigned above the others and that bishops, especially when assembled in synod or council, were along with the pope the most important repositories for ecclesiastical authority (O'Malley, 77). In other words Tierney implicitly demonstrated that the 'conciliarism' that saved the papacy at the Council of Constance could not automatically be indentified with the conciliarism that claimed a council was in every circumstance superior to the pope.

Secondly, there was the growing official realisation that democracy had much to recommend it. In his 1944 address, after Rome had been liberated from German forces, Pius XII surprised the world by commending democracy as a form of government appropriate for the time: 'Taught by bitter experience, people today more and more oppose monopolies of power that

---

6. Bernard J. F. Lonergan SJ, *Method in Theology*, London: Darton, Longman and Todd, 1975 (original 1971), 326

are dictatorial, accountable to no one, and impossible to reject. They want a system of government more compatible with the dignity and the liberty due to citizens'. He speculated that 'the future belongs to democracy'. (O'Malley, 83). Within a few years of the end of the war, all the countries of Western Europe that had been engaged in the conflict had adopted or confirmed a parliamentary form of government.

Of course the pope was not calling for such a model of governance in the church: nonetheless, by the time the Second Vatican Council met, the leaders of the majority group, both bishops and theologians, came to it with a political sense sharpened by democratic experience – and these happened to be the leaders keen on collegiality. Furthermore, in attempting to silence the new theological voices which had emerged after Vatican I, and particularly just before and after World War 2, the Holy Office had aroused the bitter resentment not just of theologians but also of some bishops, who felt that 'Rome' was overstepping its bounds (O'Malley, 88). Bishops complained that they were being treated like mere executors of the orders of the Holy See, mere *Werkzeuge*, to use Bismarck's term. What they resented as much as the punishment of theologians was the autocratic style in which it was meted out. As H.-M. Féret, one of the French Dominicans whose work was condemned, said: 'I do not see any means of reconciling with the spirit of the gospel a system that condemns someone as a result of secret denunciations, that gives the person no way of defence, and that provides no way of knowing the context of the condemnation' (O'Malley, 88). This resentment by the bishops of Roman autocracy was to surface again in the course of the Second Vatican Council.

Finally, it should be clear that, despite the liveliness of Catholic devotion and practice among the lay faithful and the emergence of charismatic leaders such as Frank Duff, still for the most part the laity were docile and passive, allowing themselves 'to be led' as Pius X put it. There was scarcely any other vision available at the time, and even well into the twentieth century in Ireland one thinks of the Unionist/Protestant fear that 'Home

Rule is Rome Rule', and the excessive deference of the state towards the Catholic Church that has been highlighted in the Ryan and Murphy reports, and that we know too well from so many other areas of our life in the not so distant past. Ironically it was an Irish Cardinal, Tomás Ó Fiaich, who noted at the 1987 Synod of Bishops that the hierarchy needed to set about 'awakening the sleeping giant' that is the laity (and, by the way, in the same speech, he also noted that 'feminism can no longer be considered middle-class madness or an American aberration' – Fahey, 334). Sadly, the church did not pay enough attention to these words and we are now faced with the consequences.

Conclusion
I have been trying to open up a little the context out of which Vatican II emerged, always with a view to a better preparation for the discernment about our situation of crisis today. I have noted that, apart from some important but relatively minimal normative content derived from sacred scripture, the life and organisation of the early church developed according to particular situations and needs. As the centuries passed, and particularly in the West, this development took a more centralised shape. How much of this is binding, is normative? How much is appropriate – perhaps, in a globalised world and in a universal church, there is real value in strong central authority, but can it be combined, as the principle of subsidiarity so central to Catholic Social Teaching (CST) recommends, with local and regional autonomy that is not simply delegation? The way the church developed owed much to secular models of government – the Roman Empire, and later imperial and monarchical structures: can it also learn from the more democratic models available today? And how much of this 'marriage between throne and altar', so characteristic of the post-Constantinian church, was consistent with the message of Jesus about 'rendering unto Caesar what is Caesar's and to God what is God's (Mk 12, 17 – used now by the church to teach the truth and value of church-state distinction)? And do present structures and institutions like the Vatican State

and the Vatican Bank[7] serve an evangelically rooted purpose or are they residual traces of past deviations?

There is a lively debate among theologians and church leaders about whether one interprets Vatican II according to a hermeneutic of continuity or discontinuity. We have seen that over the centuries, prior to Vatican II, many changes have occurred: how are we to understand these in terms of their consistency with the gospel message? Bernard Lonergan is not 'fazed' by the notion of discontinuity: rather, he is clear that doctrinal development 'often enough ... is dialectical. The truth is discovered because a contrary error has been asserted' (Lonergan, 319). Of course the Catholic claim is that certain truths have been definitively established by church councils: the question arises then as to the nature of a council and when its teaching is definitive, a question that was underlying Vatican II as it realised that in so many areas (liturgy, scripture, the separation of church and state, freedom of conscience, democracy, ecumenism, and, not least, the balancing of papal primacy with collegiality at all levels) it seemed to be in discontinuity with what went before. How free, then, are we to adapt and change our ecclesial culture and organisation, in particular in the light of the strong ecclesiological teaching of the First Vatican Council?

The church will always be in tension between its divine origin and purpose and its need to find appropriate human shape, to inculturate. And part of this inculturation will involve the need to be vigilant in face of the 'law of unintended consequences' by which actions taken for good reasons and motives may, over time, issue in deficient and even evil outcomes. The Gregorian reforms in the 11th century may well have been necessary, but their one-sided implementation over the centuries has resulted in a clericalist and papalist culture that is dysfunctional. This culture, besides stifling the proper vitality of the faithful, both

---

7. I note in this context the *Motu Proprio data* of Pope Benedict XVI on 30 December 2010 enacting laws to bring the Vatican Bank, focus of money laundering investigations in Italy, in line with international standards on financial transparency and the funding of terrorism.

women and men, and emasculating the role of bishops, is a hindrance even to the role of the papacy as a service of unity and love to all Christians. What is involved here is almost always not a criticism of persons but rather of structures and culture: but we need to go beyond the notion that just because individual bishops/priests/popes are 'nice', indeed fine people, that therefore we can leave things as they are, we can trust that all will be well. We have been alerted to deep cultural and structural flaws in our church and we need to tackle them, with or in opposition to the good people who are in positions of authority.

These are some of the issues and questions which I will go on to address through a treatment of Vatican II and the situation since. I will end this historical survey by quoting perhaps a surprising voice to sum up graphically and eloquently how the church found itself on the run-up to Vatican II. Addressing a group of young Canadian seminarians who were completing their studies in Rome in 1939, just before his death, Pope Pius XI had this to say: 'I want you to take this message away with you. The church, the Mystical Body of Christ, has become a monstrosity. The head is very large, but the body is shrunken. You, the priests, must rebuild that body of the church and the only way that you can rebuild it is to mobilise the lay people' (Orsy, 36). We turn now to examine how Vatican II tackled these issues and then, later, to analyse how its vision may be an inspiration for us in our present context.

CHAPTER THREE

The Second Vatican Council, 1962-1965
(O'Malley, chapters three on)[1]

'...but the word of God is not fettered' (2 Tim 2,:9)

Despite the underlying subversive currents of change that I have mentioned, the definitions of papal primacy and infallibility at Vatican I had persuaded some commentators that Vatican I was the 'council that ended councils' (31). Besides, on the surface at least, the church seemed to be in rude good health and there was little talk of the possibility of another council. It came as a surprise, therefore, when, just months after his election in October 1958, Pope John XXIII (the so-called caretaker pope) announced in January 1959 the convocation of a council, to be called Vatican II.

This is the council that in so many of its documents, but particularly in its *Dogmatic Constitution on the Church* (*Lumen Gentium: A Light to the Peoples*) offered us a vision in which the People of God have priority over the hierarchy (Orsy, 4) and in which *communio*/collegiality became the key note of relationships within the church. This collegiality, as treated explicitly by Vatican II, centred mainly on the relationship between the bishops and pope, but it implied also 'the question of what voice others in the church, including the laity, rightly have in decision-making' (7), so that one of the most important issues at the council became 'the desire to recognise the dignity of lay men and women and to empower them to fulfill their vocation in the church' (5).

However, this kind of outcome was not at all anticipated in the preparations for the council. This was so despite the fact

---

1. Note that all references in this chapter are to O'Malley except where otherwise indicated.

that, unlike most of the 20 councils of the past that the Catholic Church recognises as ecumenical or general councils, this one was not called to address any particular crisis. Furthermore, the pope's tone in calling the council was entirely positive (for spiritual renewal and the joy of the Christian people, and to extend the hand of friendship to separated Christian communities). Still, the prevailing assumption, operative in the 1,998 responses (to an invitation to 2,598 ecclesiastics all over the world for their views and suggestions about what should be treated at the council) was that there would be a tightening of the *status quo*, that modern evils whether inside the church or outside would be condemned, and that there would be further definitions of doctrine, especially those relating to the Virgin Mary (19-20).

General Description of the Event of the Council
It was in this context that the council convened for its first session on 11 October 1962, some 2, 500 council fathers processing for one hour, fully vested in flowing white garments with white mitres atop their heads, to attend the opening High Mass in St Peter's at which there were also in attendance theologians, non-Catholic observers and various heads of state. All of this was carried on television, and there were tens of thousands in St Peter's Square – the spectacle was magnificent. It was, O'Malley suggests, 'quite possibly the biggest meeting in the history of the world' (18). Bishops came from 116 different countries, many had a secretary or theologian with them. There were up to a 100 non-Catholic observers and, from 1963 on, a relatively small number of 'lay auditors', including some women (there were 21 men by the third period, three of whom addressed the assembly; 7 lay women and 8 from religious congregations, but none of them addressed the assembly – it should be noted that until Vatican I the presence of laity at councils was taken for granted). The central nave of St Peter's basilica was barely sufficient to hold all the attendees. Two catering stations or coffee bars (no alcohol) were set up in the basilica, and toilets were

installed both inside and outside St Peter's. There were a limited number of Public Sessions (10 in all) to which those of the general public who managed to obtain tickets were invited. Thirty seven microphones were installed. This was a gathering 'the likes of which had never been seen before' (25).

In the event, the council met in four distinct periods in the autumn of every year from 1962-1965, each period lasting about 10 weeks. The first period was under the pontificate of John XXIII, the other three under that of Paul VI. Much of the main work was done in the so-called intercessions, between the four 'sitting' periods, by bishops and theological experts (*periti*). By the end of the council, Paul VI had promulgated 16 documents in his name and in the name of the council, of different import- ance and degree of authority. The highest in rank are the docu- ments on the Liturgy, on the Church (*LG*), on Revelation, on the Church in the Modern World (*Gaudium et Spes – GS*), called 'con- stitutions'; then there were nine 'decrees' (Mass media; Catholic Eastern churches; Ecumenism; Bishops; Renewal of Religious Life; Laity; Missionary activity; Priests). Finally there were 3 'Declarations': On Christian Education; on Non-Christian Religions; and on Religious Freedom. While the distinction be- tween Constitution and the rest remains important, that be- tween Decree and Declaration has limited significance: so, for example, decrees on the Mass Media and Christian Education proved to be a lot less significant than the Declarations on Non- Christian Religions and Religious Freedom.

It should be noted that three issues were regarded as so sen- sitive or potentially explosive that Paul VI withheld them from the council's agenda – clerical celibacy, birth control, and the re- form of the Roman Curia. In addition Paul VI unilaterally created the body known as the Synod of Bishops, without providing that the council participate in its formulation. It is significant, and ironic, that these four issues continue to be a source of such controversy in the church today.

The serene tone of the final documents belies the fact that some of them were hotly, often bitterly, contested and survived only by the skin of their teeth (2). And, as in any human gathering of this nature, there all kinds of politics involved, lobbying openly and secretly, high and low moments. Somewhat surprisingly, from early on it became apparent that a majority of bishops were in favour of change on many fronts. This was shown by several early indications – first in procedural matters, when the bishops refused to accept the wishes of the Roman Curia on how things should be debated (97 and 150), and were supported by John XXIII. This was noted and resented early on by senior members of the Curia, and Cardinal Siri of Genoa, close to them, spoke of 'a certain antipathy to the Curia', deriving, he thought, from 'the eternal inferiority-complex which the Northerners have in their relations with Rome' – and, he noted in his diary, 'the devil has a hand in this' (98). The same pattern was plain in the early document on the Liturgy which, building on pre-Vatican II theological work and the wishes of many bishops, called for change and affirmed the authority of bishops and bishops' conferences to make decisions to adapt the liturgy to local circumstances, effectively nullifying canon 1257 of the Code, which placed all decisions about liturgy exclusively in the Holy See (139). Then there was the rejection (inspired, *inter alia,* by Karl Rahner and Joseph Ratzinger) of the Curia-supported text on Revelation.

Cardinals Willebrands, Frings, Bea and Suenens, among others, emerged as leaders of the group which favoured change. These were opposed by a tenacious minority, with strong roots in the Roman Curia, headed by the likes of Cardinals Ottaviani, Ruffini and the Irishman Cardinal Michael Browne.[2] Ottaviani in particular came to stand for the Curia and to embody everything that people disliked about the Holy Office (predecessor of the CDF,) and jokes about him circulated widely and began to appear in newspapers and journals – one morning, supposedly, he called a taxi and directed the driver to take him to the council – the driver hit the road for Trent (137). Ottaviani however was a formidable charac-

---

2. For a recent Irish account of Vatican II, see Bishop Michael Smith, 'An Eyewitness Account', in Dermot A. Lane and Brendan Leahy, eds, *Vatican II, Facing the 21st Century*, Dublin: Veritas, 2006, 13-30

ter, intelligent, shrewd, witty, and of unquestioned moral integrity (108), well capable of taking on opponents (as, for example, when in discussing liturgical changes, which he opposed, he said it was well and good for his opponents to quote popes like Pius XII when he agreed with their position, but what about quoting them when they did not? – 158).

However, there was of course a most serious side to all this: to obtain the kind of near unanimity that most of the documents achieved in final voting, and to satisfy the pope, this sometimes meant a certain fudging of issues, so that, for example, it has often been said with regard to our particular theme that papal primacy (Vat I) and episcopal collegiality (Vat II) were simply asserted side by side, without the higher viewpoint which might have given surer guidance for the post conciliar period. It is precisely this point of course which has led many people since to call for a third Vatican Council.

In this respect it should also be stated that while John XXIII was almost entirely non-interventionist, Paul VI was decidedly not so and there was at times great tension between him and the bishops (102-108). Related to this it would seem that the Procedures of the Council, drawn up by the Curia, with subsequent amendments of a relatively minor nature during the council, failed to make clear how the pope was to make known his own views to the bishops. They failed generally in not clearly defining the scope and limits of the authority of the various bodies responsible for different aspects of the council's business (100). This was all in the context of the unlimited discretionary authority put in the hands of the pope, faithfully reflecting Canon 222 of the Code. The council was therefore *cum et sub Petro* (with and under Peter), a living epitome of the unresolved tension between primacy and collegiality, with John understanding his role in a way which gave the council more autonomy, while Paul understood and felt his primatial responsibilities more heavily, to the point where, by the third period in 1964, his interventions left 'many, perhaps most, members of the council uncertain as to what he was up to' (107). Thus, while Paul seemed behind the general thrust of the council, he sought to introduce qualifications in a way which generated confusions, misgivings, and even distrust (107).

Yet there is no doubt that overall the council understood its role as more than consultative. It acted in accord with Canon 228 ('An ecumenical council enjoys supreme power over the universal church'), and it asserted its independence from the Roma Curia (31). The latter indeed, even early on, began to feel itself under threat as even conservative bishops, in the atmosphere of the council, began to reassess its interventions in the affairs of their dioceses and see them as high-handed (114). Yves Congar reported that by the third period all that was heard in the corridors of the Curia were bitter complaints that 'this accursed council is ruining the church' (114). Nonetheless, the Curia too could take comfort in Vatican I and also in Canon Law – Canon 222 notes that it is the right of the pope to convene and preside at a council, to determine the matters to be treated and the order to be observed, to transfer, suspend or dissolve the council and to confirm its decrees (31). Again one observes that tension between centre and periphery that O'Malley identifies as one of the three key underlying issues pervading the council (the two others are the notion of change and the style of the council) and which was addressed explicitly in the *Constitution on the Church* (*LG*), to which we will shortly turn.

The tone of the council was significantly influenced by Pope John's opening address, to which reference was often subsequently made. To those untrained in the language of papal discourse it sounded bland (94), but on more careful analysis its force and distinctive characteristics emerge. The pope distanced himself from a scolding and suspicious approach 'to the world', preferring 'the medicine of mercy rather than of severity', hoping that the church might commend itself by the validity of its teaching rather than by condemnations. At play here was the council's style of discourse, and the pope affirmed that while the fundamental teachings of the church must always remain the same, the way they are presented can change. The style, then, should be 'predominantly pastoral in character', in effect countering those who wanted Vatican II to be primarily 'doctrinal'. This spontaneous pope, full of warm humanity, who liked to tell jokes, conveyed a positive, unafraid approach to the modern world which is reflected in the documents of the council.

The Vision and Teaching of the Council in more detail

First Session, 1962 (O'Malley, chapter four)

After a contentious delay (148), during which the Melkite Maximos IV Saigh noted that Vatican I had given a partial view of the church with its emphasis on the papacy and there was need to redress the balance with a schema on the church which should be the centrepiece of the council's work, Cardinal Ottaviani introduced the schema *De Ecclesia* (About the Church) on 26 November, towards the end of the first period of the council. This text had been prepared by the Doctrinal Commission (effectively the Holy Office), one of ten commissions set up to prepare for the council. Already there had been a lot of rancour in discussion of previous texts on the council floor and the council fathers were keen at this stage to be more conciliatory in tone, even if they did express many reservations concerning *De Ecclesia*, in particular with regard to its excessively hierarchical nature, consistent with which obedience to ecclesiastical, especially papal, authority was a major preoccupation (155).

However, the Bishop of Bruges, Joseph de Smedt, was more outspoken and did not mince his words – he maintained that the text was triumphalist, clericalist and overly juridical in tone and content. Frings said it was not 'catholic': it reflected only the last 100 years, not the long history of the church and particularly its Eastern experience. A speech by Cardinal Suenens won applause: he suggested taking the theme of church as 'light to the nations', in two parts – *ad intra* and *ad extra*. Among those who supported Suenens was Cardinal Montini, later to be Paul VI, and, as O'Malley puts it, this first draft was effectively 'sent into the repair shop for what amounted to such a thorough revision that it emerged essentially a new document, *Lumen Gentium'* (7), while a second text, *Gaudium et Spes* dealt with the church and the world. As an interesting and somewhat ironic aside, it is worth noting that *Gaudium et Spes* (The Church in the Modern World) proved to be a very controversial text in the making, and Karl Rahner and Josef Ratzinger once again found themselves on the same side in arguing that it was overly-optimistic and in- carnational, without sufficient emphasis on the cross – even if, on this occasion, they lost the argument with respect to the final text.

A new co-ordinating commission gave directives that the text *De Ecclesia* was to be radically revised for the second period of the council, that the relationship between Vatican I and II, be- tween pope and bishops, the notion of episcopal collegiality – the bishops under and with Peter – should be clarified. And so, as O'Malley notes, 'collegiality would become the lightening- rod issue of the council' (163), focused of course on pope and bishops, but with enormous repercussions for all the faithful and for our vision of what it is to be church. The pre-council im- petus for a new approach came from the likes of de Lubac and Congar: and the theological advisors to the new sub-group of the Doctrinal Commission (5 bishops from the majority, 2 from the minority) included Philips, Rahner, Daniélou and, eventually, Congar (164). This meant that the drafting was taken out of the immediate hands of Ottaviani, an important turning point. Initial drafts were hotly attacked but were eventually approved by the full commission.

Second Session, 1963 (O'Malley, chapter five)
In the meantime John XXIII died and the newly elected Paul VI announced that the council would reconvene on 29 September 1963. Before the council began, the new pope addressed his for- mer curial colleagues, some 800 persons, telling them that he expected them to co-operate with the council and that it was reasonable that there would be some changes in their mode of operation. Crucially, however, he also communicated to them

that he was taking reform of the Curia off the agenda of the council – 'the reforms will be formulated and promulgated by the Curia itself' (171). This was a key strategic intervention by the pope which was to have enormous consequences for the implementation of Vatican II.

The new text on the church was introduced, four chapters on the mystery of the church, the hierarchy, the People of God (especially the laity) and the call to holiness. The strong horizontal line implicit in 'People of God', with its stress on the fundamental equality of all members of the church, had replaced the strong vertical line of ruler-subject that pervaded the original text. The style was more biblical and patristic, less juridical, with terms like communion coming to the fore (174). Significantly the new chapter four made it clear that all in the church were called to holiness, a departure from the discourse of more or less perfect forms of the Christian life.

Many issues arose in discussion, not least the proper (not delegated) authority of bishops through ordination, so that bishops were vicars of Christ and were not to be thought of as 'vicars of the Roman Pontiff' (as Leo XIII had already made clear) – the bishops, as O'Malley puts it, are not, therefore, 'heads of a branch office of the Vatican' (176). But could this be teased out further? Could, for example, canons 228 and 222 of the Code on the authority of general councils be reconciled? Should the papal prerogatives of Vatican I be repeated, be omitted, or simply put side by side with the new emphasis on collegiality?

In the course of the discussion Bishop Giuseppe Gargitter of Bolzano-Bressanone suggested that the People of God be the new chapter two, which would then be followed by the chapters on the hierarchy and laity. Suenens had already proposed this, and now it was accepted. The symbolism of the change was potent: 'the first reality of the church is horizontal and consists of all the baptised, without distinction of rank. Only then comes the vertical reality, hierarchy (178)' – this is the key insight of Vatican II on the church, and out of it comes our new vision.

The new text was winning much approval, but concerted

opposition remained, particularly to the doctrine of collegiality. Oral and written emendations came like an avalanche. The pope was besieged with different pressure groups asking him to intervene (182-3). Indicative votes were taken which showed overwhelming support for a strong notion of collegiality, helped not least by the fact that the bishops by their presence and active participation in the council had experienced collegiality, so that, as O'Malley put it, 'in principle, collegiality had achieved secure and central status in the way the church operates – or is supposed to operate' (184). The minority was tenacious, however, and continued to oppose.

Discussion at this point went on to tease out the notion of the People of God – new notes were struck by the insistence on the equality of all deriving from baptism; that the lay faithful participate in Christ's priestly, prophetic and regal mission; that the people of Christ as a whole are infallible in their faith when that faith represents a consensus – such infallibility is of course a charism that includes bishops and pope but does not rest exclusively with them; and that while Orders does introduce a divinely-ordained inequality in certain respects, still there is a validity in initiatives from below as well as from above. In this latter context the Decree on the Laity notes with approval the motif of Catholic Action concerning the 'collaboration of the laity in the apostolate of the hierarchy' (20), but balances this with their right to 'act on their own accord' (24), implying of course that what is involved is the mission or apostolate of the whole church, which cannot be equated with the mission of the hierarchy only. In the course of the lively discussion, Suenens spoke eloquently about charisms in the church and closed by making two recommendations: increasing the number of lay auditors and seeing to it that this increment included women, 'who, lest I am mistaken, make up half of the human race' (187). The schema was sent back for revision in the light of the discussion, with a vote to include a final chapter on the Blessed Virgin (instead of a separate text on Mary, wanted by many at the start of the council).

There followed a very interesting discussion on the Decree on Bishops, in which, of course, the issue of collegiality emerged once again (190-194). Maximos IV, as often, made a pertinent intervention: regarding the central government of the church he proposed a 'new solution' based on the doctrine of collegiality. The church should be governed by the successors to Peter and the other apostles, not by Peter as surrounded by the members of the Roman clergy, which was fine for the government of the diocese of Rome but not for the government of the universal church. What Maximos wanted was a radical reform in which a small group of bishops with rotating membership would always be in Rome to assist the pope in collegial fashion, mindful of his prerogatives – this group, and not the Holy Office, would be the group of government, under which the various curial Roman congregations would function and take direction. This was a proposal for an important structural change to implement practically the principle of collegiality. There followed a strong clash between Cardinal Frings and Ottaviani, widely reported in the world press, concerning how the church was to operate in the future: continue its highly centralised mode of operation, with its top-down style of management and apodictic mode of communication, or somehow attenuate them by broader consultation and sharing of responsibility. Interestingly enough, in the context of this general review of episcopal office, no attention was given to the process by which bishops were chosen – a process then, as now, shrouded in secrecy (193).

I have noted earlier that in fact Paul VI unilaterally decided not to reform the Roman Curia and, in 1965, to create the Synod of Bishops which effectively functions under the Curia: the reform of Maximos was rejected in a primatial way and the consequences remain with us today. It should also be noted of course that throughout the discussion attention was focused on the episcopal and papal dimensions of collegiality: implicit in this – and in need today of being more explicit – was the issue of lay involvement in governance, in deliberative decision making, and not just consultative, processes, as Karl Rahner would go on to talk about in the years after the council.

Third Session, 1964 (O'Malley, chapter six)
The third period reconvened on 14 September 1964. In the meantime (May 1964) the Pope had intervened by proposing thirteen 'suggestions' regarding collegiality to the Doctrinal Commission – the first major example of what came to be know as the 'red pencil' of the extraordinarily interventionist Paul VI (201). The commission considered the suggestions carefully, accepted some but rejected others, including an attempt to limit collegiality in deference to the prescriptive authority of the pope.

Lobbying continued to go on in the background, the pope being addressed by members of the minority group of bishops who feared that the church would be 'changed from monarchical to episcopalian and collegial' (202). Paul held firm for the moment, though clearly aware of the high stakes involved: 'In the end it is necessary to have faith in the consciences of the council fathers, in the force of truth, and above all in the help of the Holy Spirit', he said in a memorandum (203). In August he issued his own first encyclical, *Ecclesiam Suam* – in it he avoids touching on the issue of collegiality, refers only once to the expression 'People of God', and introduces the notion of dialogue in a way that was taken up by the council and became a *mot juste* to indicate 'the spirit' of Vatican II. I note that it does seem a little strange that Paul would issue an encyclical on a topic being currently addressed by the council, almost as if deciding by this action where the balance lay in the tension between primacy and collegiality.

The pope's opening address to the Third Period made it clear that he viewed the relationship between papal and episcopal offices as the most serious issue before the council (206). In this address he never once described the church as 'the People of God'. Cardinal Felici, Secretary-General of the Council, urged all to pay the closest attention and, as far as possible to remain in their places, driving home his point humorously by saying that the coffee bars in St Peter's would henceforth not open till 11 o'clock.

The document had now expanded to the eight chapters that we have today, but the most controversial part remained chapter three on the hierarchy, and particularly on how collegiality should be understood. There continued to be intense pressure on the pope to mitigate the notion of collegiality contained in the draft. Indicative votes again pointed to strong support for the draft as was, however, and in anticipation of a positive vote on these lines the document on bishops called in very general terms (article 5 of chapter one) for a body to make collegiality a functioning reality (along the lines proposed by Maximos and others a year earlier). In similarly general terms it called for a reform of the Curia (210). In the document on bishops that was approved in the following year the decree recommended that bishops establish in their dioceses a council made up of clergy, religious and laity to review pastoral activities in the diocese and formulate policies concerning them – the bishop was in charge, but for the first time ecclesiastical documents stressed the horizontal relationship to those over whom he presided. The document also strongly urged the creation of episcopal conferences.

Meanwhile discussion continued on other documents, including what was seen as the uncontroversial document on the laity, with the first intervention in the council by a layman, Patrick Keegan from England. There was a lively discussion on issues involved in The Church and the Modern World, including references to the topic of birth control (officially off the council agenda, with a Papal Commission set up by John XXIII in 1963). Again, the voice of Maximos Saigh was distinctive: '... there is a cleavage between the official teaching of the church and the contrary practice in most families ... let me speak frankly: do not the official positions of the church in this matter require revision in the light of modern research – theological, medical, psychological, sociological?' (237). Suenens was even more dramatic and direct: 'I plead with you brothers. We must avoid another "Galileo case". One is enough for the church' (238). The pope was angry with these interventions, which got a lot of media attention.

There began then a troubled time for Paul VI in his relationship with the council (from early November on). Unusually he attended a working session of the council to commending a schema on the missions, which did not, however, win council approval – Paul was mortified (239). And now, in mid November, renewed controversy broke out about two of the most controverted texts – on the church and on religious liberty. Paul intervened in several ways at this point, postponing the vote on religious liberty, sending nineteen emendations to the Decree on Ecumenism, and communicating a 'Preliminary Explanatory Note' (*Nota Explicativa Praevia*) for *LG* that interpreted the meaning of collegiality in chapter three.

Paul's actions caused deep distress to the great majority of bishops and fuelled suspicions 'that a small number of council fathers were using him as a tool to attain what they could not attain through the deliberations in St Peter's' (241). The bishops were angry and frustrated, including the American bishops in particular over the delay about religious liberty. In fact, on this text, in retrospect commentators judge Paul's decision positively – the revised text was a better one, and was approved the following year (242). His intervention re ecumenism is judged less favourably: the emendations did not alter the test significantly, and did not win over those who fiercely opposed the decree.

The intervention in *LG* was altogether a more substantive matter. The Preliminary Note was intended to be the norm by which chapter three on collegiality was to be interpreted. Resentment flared – at the last-minute timing (this was the last working week of this period of the council), at the impossibility of any public discussion, and especially at the autocratic and coy implications of Felici's announcement of the Note as coming 'from a higher authority' – it came in fact from the Doctrinal Commission, but ordered by the pope. The substance of the note was very technical and its interpretative status disputed: most commentators shared the opinion of Philips (main author) that the Note did not change the meaning of the document, and, shortly after the council, Joseph Ratzinger substantially agreed but, nonetheless, found this 'a very intricate text', marked by ambivalence and ambiguities and saw it as tipping the balance in favour of primacy (244).

In any case the minority was ecstatic and it won their support for the final approval of the text (only 5 negative votes out of 2,156 cast). But, as O'Malley says, 'the price for that virtual unanimity was high. No matter what the pope hoped to accomplish, he in fact gave those who opposed collegiality a tool they could – and would – use to interpret the chapter as a reaffirmation of the *status quo*. If there was anything about the Note that gave the leaders of the majority pause, it was the ready, even gleeful, support the doctrine of collegiality now received from council fathers who had done everything they could to scuttle it' (245).

The document was publicly promulgated at the end of the third period on Saturday 21 November 1964. At this ceremony the pope claimed that, in reference to *LG*, 'no change is made in traditional teaching', and, curiously, that the character of the church was 'both monarchical and hierarchical' where in reality the terms 'both primatial and collegial' seemed called for – monarch does not occur a single time in *LG* or in any of the texts of the council (245). The pope went on to declare Mary to be 'Mother of the Church' – again, a unilateral declaration, opposed to what the council had decided. Philips judged the declaration a deliberate assertion by the pope of his primacy (245). Paul's face was grim at this ceremony: no one doubted that this last week had seriously damaged the relationship between the pope and the assembly (245).

Fourth Session, 1965 (O'Malley, chapter seven)
Paul VI opened the fourth period (14 September 1965) with a speech whose tone was altogether positive. And he had two surprise announcements – an impending trip to the United Nations

and then the creation of the Synod of Bishops. The latter was of crucial strategic importance – issued the same day in a *Motu Proprio* called *Apostolica Solicitudo* (*AS*) it was initially received positively – it seemed like a response to the desire to govern collegially, to internationalise the Curia. But closer scrutiny revealed something else: the document stated that in every particular the Synod was subject 'immediately and directly' to the power of the pope. It was strictly an advisory body with no authority beyond what the pope conceded to it – this was in effect an expression of papal primacy, not collegiality, a pre-emptive strike by the centre: 'The body described in *AS* could hardly have been further from what Maximos had proposed the previous year. With one stroke the text cut collegiality off from grounding in the institutional reality of the church' (252-3).

The commission on bishops had little choice but to incorporate the substance of the pope's intervention into article 5 of their text on bishops, thereby undermining the more radical proposals of the likes of Maximos and Lercaro. Cardinal Suenens thought at the time that the Synod might eventually issue directives even to the Curia, but two months later he came to believe that the pope would not make serious use of it (252).

This fourth period witnessed many passionate debates, in particular on Religious Liberty, Revelation and The Church in the Modern World – some of the best sound-bites again coming from Maximos, who in a letter to Paul VI about clerical celibacy (priests in his rite could marry) noted that 'this problem exists and is becoming daily more difficult. It cries out for a solution … Your Holiness knows well that repressed truths turn poisonous' (272).

As the final texts began to be approved Paul, in a public address on 18 November, began to reveal the steps he himself was taking the ensure the council's implementation, including some changes in the Roman Curia even if, he said, 'there are no serious reasons for changing its structures' (283). Paul also made it clear that it would be the Curia who would have the main responsibility in the post-council period for the implantation of the conciliar decrees. In an audience with the pope, Suenens said that the bishops feared the consequences after the council of an unreformed Curia, especially if the major personalities remained the same, but he was interrupted by the pope who defended the Curia and said that no major changes were needed. (283). In the same public address Paul, again curiously, spoke in a way which highlighted the prerogatives of the papacy, despite this being a council at which collegiality was a central and defining issue. Nonetheless the general body of bishops was more conscious of achievement, the battles had been fought, and they were keen also to get back to their dioceses.

But in reality there were still more battles to be fought. The pope intervened again by insisting on a change in *GS* which would make explicit a clear rejection of contraceptives. There was much to-ing and fro-ing behind the scenes, and Felici reported that among the things Paul said was that 'if others had their consciences, he had his' (285). In the event it was communicated finally that the pope's intervention was in the nature of '*modi*', counsels, and that they should be treated like the *modi* of any other bishop. Slight modifications were made to the text, but no explicit condemnation of contraceptives was mentioned. This was yet another example of the lack of clarity in the relationship between pope and bishops.

The final documents were carried with big majorities and the council ended with a public session on 7 December and a final ceremony on 8 December at the end of which the crowd of about 300,000 broke into applause and cheers.

Summary vision
The vision of church that emerged from the council was that of church as *communio*, a union of persons in a unique sense – created by the Holy Spirit. This communion is originally present in the inner life of God, one God in three persons, unity in diversity or diversity in unity. The church is a mystery or sacrament (light for the world), a sign, of this divine *communio*, and all external manifestations of this organic communion or union of

minds and hearts, such as collegiality and solidarity, flow from this original vision. In this context the focus is first on the whole People of God, all of whom are called to intimate union with God and to holiness. The lay faithful, then, share in the priestly, prophetic and kingly role of Jesus Christ both within the church and in the secular world outside. It is the People of God as a whole in whom resides the charism of inerrancy in faith. It is within this, subordinate, context that the role of the hierarchy, including that of papacy, is to be understood: these elements exist to serve the whole People of God, not the other way around (McBrien, 166).

This, then, is not a military organisation where the highest in rank command and the others obey (Orsy, 8) – the notion of *communio* pertains to all levels of ecclesial life, based on the common gift of baptism possessed by all, so that authority is to be exercised within the call to be of one mind and heart, and with respect for the inherent rights of the faithful, priests, bishops and pope. Local churches are each the Body of Christ in their own places; they are not simply administrative subdivisions of the one, universal church (McBrien, 191). Papal primacy is a primacy of service and unity, and the papal office must respect the legitimate diversity of the church as a communion of local churches and practice a collegial mode of decision making (McBrien, 101). Finally, the church is not itself the kingdom of God but is there to serve the kingdom, and the Body of Christ is composed of more than Catholics.

All this is a huge shift from the dominant hierarchical and overly-juridical vision that was dominant before the council, but in large parts it is a shift that we have not yet effected. The baptised faithful, the laity, are in some sense still the amateurs, while the 'real church', in the mentalities of too many people, is the hierarchy. One does not get a sense, for example, of a church which has internalised the kind of vision which would entail authoritative teachers listening carefully, in servant mode (the *Magisterium* is 'not above the word of God but acts as its servant' – 227, quoting *Dei Verbum* 10), to that indefectibility to be found in the 'sense of the faithful' and the whole People of God (*LG*,

12) in the proper exercise of their *Magisterium*. Nor does one get a sense of a genuinely collegial mode of governance, respectful of the principle of subsidiarity so central to Catholic Social Teaching, and distancing itself from a more pyramid model of hierarchical governance.

We all need conversion to come to terms with the implications of this vision. The church is a co-operative body with the aim of being united in mind and heart, and we must take our responsibility for this by not exaggerating proper respect for pastors and leaders into a cult of personality or a culture of unthinking deference (Orsy, 12). And so we are at a delicate moment, as I indicated earlier, quoting Orsy – conversions all round are needed and our aim must be 'to search for better balances without damaging vital forces' (12). The transition from insights to practice, from vision to legislation takes time: we are in this time now. Nourished by this new vision we must continue with the search, begun in Vatican II, for the appropriate external structures and norms (including legal ones) to express, promote and sustain the internal bond of communion.[3]

Concluding Reflections
It is one thing to have a vision, another to know how to and to actually implement it. The majority side in Vatican II 'assumed an easier translation of ideas from the scholars' study to the social reality of the church than proved to be the case' (292). Even before the council ended in 1965 there was a discrepancy between what the bishops hoped they had accomplished and what had happened. The majority was consistently frustrated in its efforts to make its will felt through the establishment of real structural changes. It sometimes seemed to think that winning the affirmation of certain principles in the face of opposition to them would

3. The observations of Brendan Leahy are apt in this context: 'The need to promote a culture of synodality is one of the signposts along the journey of reception of the Second Vatican Council's ecclesiological focus on communion. But it is also the case that dissatisfaction has been expressed at how this synodal praxis had been realised', in Lane and Leahy eds, op cit, 65

ensure their implementation (312). On this issue of the centre-periphery (the balance between the primatial and collegial elements) the minority never really lost control (311) – with the aid of Paul VI they held firm and steady and in the decades afterwards became even stronger. The contest was unequal – the council was held at the centre, organised by the centre, to be implemented by the centre. The Synod of Bishops, as conceived by Paul, 'severed collegiality, the doctrine empowering the periphery, from institutional grounding' (311) – it ended up as an abstract teaching without point of entry into the social reality of the church – it ended up an ideal, no match for the deeply entrenched system' (311).

And, I would add, there is still work to be done on a clarification of the vision itself and the principles and ideas which inform it: if nothing is taken away from the power of the pope as defined by Vatican I, how can there be proper (and not simply delegated) power of bishops, individually and as a group, through ordination, from God, and not just from papal permission? Of course it is the case that there will always be a tension between centre and periphery (in both secular and ecclesiastical spheres). This is due to the human complexity of government for which there is no simple, ideal solution. Nonetheless it is clear that the vision and teaching of Vatican II intended to invite us to a new way of imagining and being church, which we have only begun to implement, and from which in ways we have regressed. The crisis in the church today is calling on us to reconsider this vision, to clarify it and to seek for appropriate instruments of implementation.

This clarification of principles will also hopefully aim for a deeper understanding of the development of doctrine, difficulties around which are hinted at in the theological buzz-words of today –viz a hermeneutic of continuity (legitimate reform, in Vatican discourse) or discontinuity (rupture, in Vatican discourse) . Richard McBrien, for one, speaks of these two tendencies as complementary rather than contradictory (McBrien, 199).

In this context it is interesting to observe that one of the ways the majority tried to argue for the validity of their vision of a less monarchical, hierarchical church was to use the notion of *ressourcement* (going back to the sources), saying in effect that they were more conservative, more in continuity with the tradition than the conservatives themselves. They were, of course, asking a great deal of the minority – the adoption of a new mind-set and a new value system, the acceptance of assumptions they feared and abhorred (292-3). Ironically, since the time of the council, it is very often the 'progressives' who interpret the council according to a hermeneutic of discontinuity, the conservatives who claim continuity, because in fact, as lived out in the church, the more hierarchical model has continued to dominate.

Indeed one of the major underlying issues throughout the council was how to deal with change. Newman famously said: 'In a higher world it is otherwise, but here below to live is to change, and to be perfect is to have changed often'.[4] This arose at the council due to the keener sense of history developed since the nineteenth century, the abandonment of that classicist worldview to which we have already referred (37 –with references to Lonergan and Collingwood). And this was the way John XXIII approached the council, putting *aggiornamento*, up dating, on the agenda by stating that it was part of its purpose (299), a purpose taken on by the council also in terms of reading 'the signs of the times'. Already this notion of *aggiornamento* went beyond the siege mentality of the Long Nineteenth Century: it meant a less defensive attitude to the modern world, the end of integralism, it meant more than using modern inventions like microphones and TV but also appropriating certain cultural assumptions and values.

The two other terms used to tease out this issue were development and *ressourcement*. Development seemed the least threatening, implying continuity, progress, evolution. But could development of doctrine go beyond previous teaching in a way that seemed to (or really did) contravene it? (9). And updating

---

4. Newman, *Development of Christian Doctrine*, 40 – from Mansfield, op cit, 65

was fine up to a point (for example, the abolition of the benefice system for clerical recompense), but how far could one go? How, for example, could the categories of development or *aggiornamento* satisfy the kind of change involved in the Decree on Religious Liberty with its focus on separation of church and state and freedom of conscience? In such cases the notion of *ressourcement* proved more useful – the historicality of modernity knew that things were not always as they are now, that by returning to the past one could retrieve something more appropriate or more authentic to the present situation (300-1). This was of particular relevance to a church whose identity and self-understanding depends not just on being able to adapt to present needs and pastoral situations but also in being faithful to what it understands as a God-given revelation as to its constitution.

This use of *ressourcement* was what was driving *LG*, in particular chapter three on hierarchy/collegiality. In particular, *ressourcement* was the principle that validated collegiality (43). The church of the first millennium functioned collegially, even if the leadership role of Rome was also a venerable tradition (10). It was also true of course, as already stated, that many of the bishops at Vatican II had been influenced by political democracy, which had been praised by both Popes John and Paul. And so, in a sense, there was a locking of horns in Vatican II, in the collegiality debate, between change understood as *ressourcement* and as development: the latter, in the West, in particular in the nineteenth century, seemed to suggest the legitimacy of a monarchical papacy; the former seemed to retrieve a collegiality that had atrophied in practice but in theory was now more attuned to the democratic spirit of the age.

The majority placed the two side by side at Vatican II as compatible, as they had been in a much earlier era: in their view collegiality was, indeed, an enhancement of papal primacy and an aid to its functioning (303). But the minority (many of them from the Curia) saw this kind of *ressourcement* as a threat to the authentic development represented by Vatican I, smacking of conciliarism, making the church unworkable, incompatible with papal primacy which they often seemed to understand in Bismarck's terms as an absolute monarchy possessing all authority in the church. Collegiality was the supreme instance in the council of the effort to moderate the centralising tendencies of the ecclesiastical institution, of the effort to give those from the periphery a more authoritative voice not just back home but also at the centre (303). And the collegiality spoken about of bishops and pope was symptomatic of a more general trend to promote collegial relationships throughout the church, extending to priests and laity as well (304-5).

All this had to do with style also. John XXIII wanted a pastoral council, and the fathers responded by being more biblical and patristic than juridical. But the main characteristic of this new style was that it was dialogical, its rhetoric was not juridical or legislative, it was intent on winning inner assent to truths and values rather than prescribing them (306). The council in this sense was a language-event (epideictic or panegyric, not apodictic), an enormous break from the legislative and juridical model that had prevailed since Nicea (11 – a language of 'public order', of power words – 45), encapsulating a preference for one of two visions as summed up in couplets like from command to invitation, from law to ideals, from definition to mystery, from threats to persuasion, from coercion to conscience, from monologue to dialogue, from ruling to serving, from withdrawn to integrated, from vertical to horizontal, from exclusion to inclusion … (307). Of course what was involved here was not a repudiation of the other term of the couplet, the other vision, but a better balance.

This was a style less autocratic and more collaborative, listening, eager to find common ground, assuming innocence until guilt is proven, eschewing secret oaths, anonymous denunciations and inquisitorial tactics (308-9). O'Malley judges that this style or spirit is central to the interpretation of the council ('the hermeneutical key *par excellence*' 49), which was calling for a better balance between order (law, authority, the centre) and charism (inspiration, initiative, the periphery – 11). This style or spirit is collegial, and one of its specific contents was precisely the teaching on collegiality. Its context is one which easily allows talk of holiness – the documents of Vatican II are religious documents in a way that is without precedent in conciliar documents, and no previous council has ever explicitly asserted the idea that the church is all about holiness (51). This notion of style adds substance to the belief of the council fathers themselves that something deeply important had happened at Vatican II – what O'Malley terms 'a significant break with the past' – (McBrien, 202). This kind of style, applied to leadership, meant that the council wanted to move away from a mode of governance that 'ignored or badly minimised the horizontal traditions of Catholicism' to one that should function 'with a respect for conscience that transformed the members of the church from 'subjects' into participants' – the church 'like all good teachers, needed to learn as it taught' (O'Malley, as quoted by McBrien, 204).

Apart, then, from the failure to implement the vision, it would seem that the vision itself needs some clarification: how, more precisely, is primacy to be defined in such a way as to offer strong leadership without stifling local autonomy? How can checks and balances be introduced to make the church function less as a 'closed' organisation, more as an 'open' one? How can leadership at all levels – episcopal, presbyteral, faithful – be empowered? How, above all, can we balance doctrine and dogma with the requirements of our own pastoral situation, as the early church was able to respond to the real needs of their day?

CHAPTER FOUR

After Vatican II up to today

We have noted that something really important happened at Vatican II, and yet there were deficiencies, especially with regard to implementation. The point can be well illustrated by a personal anecdote. My brother, then about 17, asked our local priest in Clontarf if he, as a layman, could help out in the parish. The priest was dumbfounded: what did my brother mean?

In an interesting new book[1] Michael Paul Gallagher notes how important the imagination is in the thinking of many religious explorers – for example, Newman, Charles Taylor, Flannery O'Connor, von Balthasar, Dorothy Soelle, and Pierangelo Sequeri. It is time to imagine something different for our church. This, too, is the message of distinguished canonist Ladislas Orsy – yes, certainly we need better management and communications structures, but above all we need a different vision, we need to stretch our imaginations, to allow ourselves be converted and have that 'baptised imagination' which Gabriel Daly often spoke about.

The vision need not be created *ex nihilo* – it will be along the lines of Vatican II, with appropriate adjustments for the signs of our times and with appropriate institutional grounding to make up for the deficiencies of Vatican II in this area. We are not simply 'stuck' with the seemingly commonsense model of church that we have now. As Lonergan notes, common sense is useful but limited: it is subject to bias and, unless questioned and critically examined, can in fact be common nonsense: '… common sense commonly feels itself omnicompetent … and commonly is

1. M.P. Gallagher, *Faith Maps*, London: Darton, Longman and Todd, 2010

unaware of the admixture of common nonsense in its more cherished convictions and slogans'.[2]

The fall-out from the clerical child sexual abuse scandal has shown us that our current model of church is nonsense, and we have an important and urgent responsibility to address this issue. This is the nonsense referred to by Pius XI in 1939 when he noted that the church had become 'a monstrosity', in that 'the head is very large, but the body is shrunken'. In theory this was rectified by the ecclesiology of Vatican II, but, as we have seen, the council did not provide sufficiently for the practical implementation of the theory. It will not do to minimise the issue by simply saying that God had promised to be with the church always, to the end of time: this ignores the simple reality that God has not promised to be with the church in Ireland till the end of time; that, for example, the once vibrant church in North Africa has long since disappeared (and it happened before the emergence of Islam), and that, more importantly, God's promises always call forth a human response.

Part One: Post –Vatican II (McBrien, parts seven and eight)[3]
Even after the non-collegial publication of *Humanae Vitae* in 1968 we find Karl Rahner, in the early 1970s (1972), still hoping that the new church envisaged by Vatican II might become a reality.[4] Rahner notes that the supreme and permanent power of jurisdiction of the pope for the whole church, as defined in Vatican I, 'is not simply identical with the whole gigantic administrative machinery which has developed historically and continues to exist and operate up to the present time in Rome'. He goes on to say that the pope can and should allow that more belongs to the autonomous competence of particular churches, including a greater say in the governance of the universal

2. B. J. F. Lonergan, op cit, 53
3. References in this Part One will be to McBrien, except where otherwise indicated.
4. See O'Hanlon, *Studies*, 2010, 289-292 with reference to K. Rahner, 'Structural Change in the Church of the Future', available in *Theological Investigations*, vol 20, London: DLT, 1981, 115-132

church, and more responsibility in the appointment of bishops. He seeks a real internationalisation of the Roman Curia. He argues that bishops too often see themselves as governing their dioceses in the name of the pope, not of Christ, and that, instead, they ought to take appropriate spiritual, administrative and teaching initiatives which need not always be 'positively supported by Roman approval, merely because these questions have their importance elsewhere in the church'. Of course the bishop must 'live in unity and peace with Rome', but Rahner is sketching a much more responsible and assertive role for the individual bishop and the regional college of bishops. He goes on to argue 'for more democratic structures' that would give better expression to the collaboration of all the faithful in the life of the church and in its 'decisions of authority', for lay participation in decision making to be more than informal, to be enshrined in juridical and visible structures that do not depend simply on the goodwill of office-holders.[5]

But sadly, as Bishop Joseph Duffy said (2010), our church has 'not embraced the great reform that was brought about by Vatican II.'[6] He was speaking about Ireland, but he might have been speaking more widely. It is true there were significant positive changes – liturgy in the vernacular and the heightened visibility of the role of the non-ordained in the life of the church are two examples that come readily to mind. And so, for example, in the USA, the lay faithful work in chanceries, ecclesiastical courts, parish councils and other ministries, and here in Ireland too we have lay-readers, ministers of the Eucharist and so on.

But, as Ladislas Orsy notes[7] on a whole host of issues the thrust of the council, far from being implemented, has actually

---

5. See also Karl Rahner, *The Dynamic Element in the Church*, London: Burns and Oates, 1964, 71-73 on the 'democratic' Church.

6. In an interview with Michael Kelly, *Irish Catholic*, 25 March 2010. In this context it is interesting to note that respondents to the 'structured dialogue' around the papal letter in 2010 speak of the need to 'relight the vision of Vatican II' – Bishop Seamus Freeman, *The Irish Times*, Tuesday, 28 December 2010

7. O'Hanlon, *Studies*, 2010, 292-300 with reference to Orsy's *Receiving the Council*.

been reversed. And so, for example, the revised Code of Canon Law (1983) not only fails to vindicate the rights of the faithful as articulated by Vatican II, in one important respect it actually reverses even the pre-Vatican II situation (in its exclusion, in Canon 129, of the laity from any major decision-making processes). Similarly, with respect to bishops and their conferences, instead of the empowerment that Vatican II envisaged, what has happened for the most part is that intermediate bodies and persons have been weakened while Rome has strengthened its control – Episcopal Conferences, for example, have no genuine corporate power according to the *Motu Proprio* of John-Paul II *Apostolicos Suos* (1998). This Letter allows for 'affective' but not 'effective' collegiality. And in another *Motu Proprio* from the same year (*Ad tuendam fidem* – to protect the faith, 1998), according to Orsy, a new category of defined teaching ('definitely taught') is introduced. This reinforces the sense of 'creeping infallibility' that Congar spoke of, especially since, in an accompanying commentary, examples of such teaching (claimed to be 'irreformable', while not strictly infallible) include the invalidity of Anglican Orders and the non-ordination of women. All this occurs in a context where justice is scarcely done within the church in terms of ecclesiastical procedure for handling offences in doctrinal matters – Orsy examines the 1997 rules and says: 'A conclusion emerges in stark simplicity: … the Regulations do not respond, as they were intended, to the demands of the present day … they were not born from the vision of human dignity and the respect for honest conscience that is demanded in the world over today' (Orsy, 102-103 and all of chapter seven).

This overall reversal happened despite some official teaching and strong theological opinion which pointed in a different direction (278ff). So, for example, the Extraordinary Synod of 1985, to celebrate the 20th anniversary of Vatican II, noted that because the church is a communion 'there must be participation and corresponsibility at all of the church's levels' (283). And if the extraordinarily charismatic papacy of John-Paul II – in tandem with globalisation and enhanced communications technology – served to deepen the centralisation of papal authority to the detriment of the authority of the other bishops and local churches (298), still it was this same pope in 1995 who asked for help 'in heeding the request made of me to find a way of exercising the primacy which, while in no way renouncing what is essential to its mission, is nonetheless open to a new situation' (299). He went on to pray 'for the Holy Spirit to shed his light upon us, enlightening all the pastors and theologians of our churches that we may seek – together of course – the forms in which this ministry may accomplish a service of love recognised by all concerned ... this is an immense task, which we cannot refuse and which I cannot carry out by myself' (Orsy, 11).

In response, retired Archbishop of San Francisco Archbishop John Quinn published a study in 1999, based on a lecture given in 1996, in which he judged that the pope's declaration that primatial responsibilities are to be fulfilled in communion with the whole college of bishops would imply that 'the normal mode of the exercise of papal authority will be collaborative and consultative, one that respects legitimate church structures such as the patriarchates and episcopal conferences, and one that is dedicated to preserving diversity within the framework of unity' (300). In his conclusion Quinn writes that 'two things, more than others, are the greatest problem for the church and for Christian unity. The first is centralisation; the other, the need for reform of the Roman Curia ... Once the decision is made to move towards decentralisation', following the lead of large international corporations, 'the substantial reform of the Roman Curia will be inevitable' (300). He went on to say, about the pope's invitation for a reconsideration of his role, that 'If there is too much delay, too much diffidence, the time will pass. It is imperative not to lose this moment of grace' (301) – words which, indeed, might apply to our situation today.

Cardinal Danneels (1997) likewise weighed in, proposing that the church 'should now begin a broad process of decentralisation', noting the discrepancy between the first and second millennium exercise of papal primacy. The Roman Curia should be 'an instrument of the pope and nothing more'; it too often acts as 'a command organisation that assumes part of the authority of the pontiff' (301). In *The Tablet* in 1999 Cardinal König, a veteran of Vatican II, also proposed decentralisation, stating that the Roman Curia 'remains a powerful force tending in the opposite direction, towards centralism'. It has 'appropriated the task of the episcopal college'. According to König subsidiarity (*Quadragesimo Anno*, 1931, Pius XI) is the key to this discussion – nothing should be done at a higher level that can be done better or equally well at a lower level, and Pius XII in his Christmas address of 1946 applied this principle not only to society but to the church itself (302-303).

The voices of these official figures were reinforced by many theological opinions. The influential German ecclesiologist Pottmeyer notes that 'listening to what the churches are saying is, in fact, an earmark of the ministry of unity (papacy)' and implies the episcopal body and the sense of the faithful. He goes on to argue that a centralist papacy can only become a papacy in communion 'if it normally makes no decrees or decisions affecting the universal church without formally inviting the input of the local churches and their bishops'. He roots all this in an understanding of what Jesus was doing in proclaiming the reign of God and in the notion of the church as a sign or sacrament of this reign. In this perspective 'the strongest argument against a centralistic, authoritarian papacy appeals not to democracy, human rights or liberal claims, but to Jesus' promise of God's new creation' (305).

We have already noted the voice of church historian John O'Malley. McBrien (305-7) cites an article written by O'Malley for *America* in 2000 where he notes that even until the time of Luther 'relatively few Christians knew that the papacy existed, and surely only a minuscule percentage believed it had anything to do with the way they lived their lives ...' O'Malley goes on to contrast this with the situation of today when for Catholics it is the pope who 'runs the church', obedience to his teachings and practical decrees is taken as a measure of one's fidelity. He makes all episcopal appointments (as recently as 1829, of 648 diocesan bishops in the Latin church, only 24 were appointed by the pope!) and bishops serve as his personal representatives in their respective dioceses. O'Malley goes on to note that 'it is a rare Catholic rectory, chancery office, or bishop's residence that does not have a framed portrait of the current pope hanging prominently in the building' (306). He judges that this phenomenon which he calls 'papalisation' is 'the most important change' that has occurred in the life and practice of the Catholic Church in contrast to earlier times – the papalisation of Catholicism, indeed, is 'the change of the millennium' (305).

North American ecclesiologist Avery Dulles (308-310) is a dissenting voice to the counter-trends we have just outlined. It is instructive to listen to the reasons why. He, also in an article for *America* in 2000, unlike O'Malley, celebrates the 'papalisation' of Catholicism, particularly under John-Paul II. He does so because he believes that the 'globalisation' of the papacy in the past two centuries has been a positive development for the Catholic Church, especially for its unity. What others see as deficiencies in John-Paul II's papal style Dulles views as assets. Where others reinforce the principle of subsidiarity in opposition to the recentralisation of authority in the Vatican, Dulles argues that 'local questions often have ramifications for the universal church, and therefore require the involvement of higher authority'. Against those who have advocated a return to synodal models of church governance, Dulles notes that the patriarchates often quarrelled among themselves and the Orthodox Church today is 'plagued by rivalries among the autocephalous churches of Eastern Europe'. Over against the stated importance of national episcopal conferences, he reminds us of the dangers of nationalism and how the resurgence of Roman authority in the nineteenth century was a 'signal benefit' in this regard. While not advocating a return to the pre-Vatican II situation, Dulles clearly sees it as the responsibility of the 'Roman centre' to hold everything in balance. He seems to advocate a purely consultative role to intermediate bodies and persons, and he op-

poses efforts to strengthen the role of national episcopal conferences and to reform the Roman Curia in order to weaken its centralised power over the local bishops. Given the global character
of the Catholic Church today and the rapidity of modern communications, Dulles concludes, the church needs a stronger, not
a weaker, papacy.

One notes the contrast here with the position of Karl Rahner,
who shared Dulles' view that now, for the first time in history,
the church had the opportunity to become operationally (and not
just in theory) universal, a world church ('global'), but who also
believed that this should happen in a way which respected and
empowered local autonomy at all levels (350-1).[8] The position of
Dulles, however, has the merit of alerting us to the complexity
of the situation and to the merits of strong central leadership in
a globalised world. It is interesting to recall how such a seemingly mundane new reality as the railway was such a significant
factor in enabling the centralisation stressed by Vatican I, how
television and enhanced communications brought our world
further together by Vatican II, and now how the internet has further realised McLuhan's prophecy of the world as the 'global
village'. In this context it is understandable that the call in economic circles is for more effective global leadership, and it would
be ironic if we, members of a universal world-church, were to
look the papal gift-horse in the mouth. Cambridge historian
Eamon Duffy writes wisely on this issue. He notes the value of
the papacy in embodying continuity with the past in terms of
apostolicity and in holding things together in the present in

---

8. 'While Rahner believed that the Council had opened new possibili-
ties in the relationship between local churches and "the centre", his reflections on life in the Church after Vatican II concluded that the relationship between the Pope and the bishops remained too strongly
weighted in favour of the central authority. To the end of his life, therefore, Rahner continued to advocate that the Pope should take action
both to limit his own authority and to give practical expression to the
fact that the bishops were more than advisors to the Pope' – Richard
Lennan, 'Ecclesiology and Ecumenism', in Declan Marmion and Mary
E. Hines, eds, *The Cambridge Companion to Karl Rahner*, Cambridge
University Press, 128-143, at 138

terms of unity. This unity cannot always be maintained simply by means of the force of persuasion and good example – there is need too of the authority of office and, arguably, it is this authority that, for example, acts as the 'strongest glue holding the centrifugal energies of American Catholicism in some sort of unity' (76).[9]

Nonetheless Duffy is clear as well that the papacy in its present form is overly-dominant, to the detriment of the proper autonomy of local churches and to the making of space for all the others form of leadership which are given as part of the sacrament of Baptism.[10] And so we do need to address the pope's own invitation for reform and the vision of Vatican II for greater collegiality. Secular polities encounter some of this same complexity of course – how does one exercise strong central leadership in a way that does not emasculate the autonomy of regions? One notes, in this context, the federal model of the United States, the looser arrangement of the EU, the relationship in our state between national and local government, and the global entity that is the United Nations.

Writing again in 2000 in *America*, Ladislas Orsy (309-312) rebuts Dulles, saying that Dulles is too complacent about the *status quo* and in this respect does not honour the pope's own invitation in *Ut Unum Sint* (1995). Orsy argues that the centre has become strong at the expense of the weakness of the 'provinces' and that to strengthen communion eight specific areas need attention: the universal church and the particular churches, sub-

9. Eamon Duffy, *Faith of Our Fathers*, London/New York: Continuum, 2004, 76; and chs 7-9 for Duffy's further reflections.
10. The remarks of James Corkery and Thomas Worcester in this context are apt: 'Certainly the papacy enjoys a stature in the world today that it could never have acquired without the modern means of communication. However, its use of these has also made it so central, so centralising, a force in Roman Catholic life that its gains *ad extra* are matched by losses *ad intra* as more and more Catholics –from bishops to ordinary believers, not to mention women, theologians, homosexuals, and victims of sexual abuse by clergy and religious – find themselves increasingly alienated from a centralised church that has forgotten that Rome is not the only player.' – Corkery and Worcester, op cit, 248-249

sidiarity, collegiality, the appointment of bishops, episcopal conferences, the Synod of Bishops, papal teaching (in particular the ambiguity of the term 'definitive' teaching that has arisen since the pontificate of John Paul II and the sense that this theologically ambiguous term is being used more and more to enforce doctrinal declarations) and the Roman Curia. In developing his position he notes that it would have made no sense for Vatican II to have affirmed collegiality, nor would there have been any fierce debate over it at the council, if all it meant, as Avery Dulles seems to assume, is 'mere consultation'. On the contrary, Orsy insists, 'collegiality means participation in the act of decision, as it happens precisely at an ecumenical council' (310). He goes on to note that 'in the practical order, episcopal conferences exist and operate at the good pleasure of the Holy See', which is not true to the notion of proper episcopal authority as taught in Vatican II. Similarly the Synod of Bishops remains a consultative body only.

The Congregation for the Doctrine of the Faith (CDF) itself issued a document on papal primacy in 1998, as a response to Pope John-Paul II's 1995 invitation. It noted that the Petrine ministry is 'not an office of co-ordination or management, nor can it be reduced to a primacy of honour or conceived as a political monarchy' (313-4). The primacy is one of service, subject to the Word of God, and exercised in communion with the bishops, so that 'listening to what the churches are saying is, in fact, an earmark of the ministry of unity. It is a consequence also of the unity of the episcopal body and of the *sensus fidei* of the entire people of God'. It goes on to say that 'the fact that a particular task has been carried out by the primacy in a certain area does not mean by itself that this task should necessarily be reserved always to the Roman pontiff; and vice-versa. Discerning the appropriate ways to exercise the primacy requires the assistance of the Holy Spirit and fraternal dialogue between the bishop of Rome and the other bishops.' One notes here the introduction of the entirely proper notion of the servant characteristic of primacy, true to the vision of Vatican II. However one also notes that unless this notion of service is effectively institutionalised – by, for example, legally empowering decision making at local level and insisting on collegial structures at primatial level – it can be used as a rhetorical cloak for patterns of behaviour and power that are authoritarian and far from servant-like.

Of significant interest in this whole discussion is the experience of other Christian churches and the several ecumenical statements that have emerged, including ARCIC II (1999), in which the *sensus fidelium* is stressed: 'In each community there is an exchange, a mutual give and take, in which bishops, clergy and lay people receive from as well as give to others within the whole body' (318). The bishops need to be alert to the *sensus fidelium*, they need to consult the faithful (319). The document goes on to acknowledge that the primacy exercised by the Bishop of Rome is a 'specific ministry concerning the discernment of truth', but exercised always within, not outside or over against, the college of bishops, a primacy which will assist the church on earth to be the authentic catholic *koinonia* (*communio*) in which unity does not curtail diversity, and diversity does not endanger but enhances unity' (321).

Last, but by no means least, in this quick survey of developments since Vatican II, I note the significant contribution of feminist theologians and ecclesiologists. Mary Hines notes that 'ecclesiology is perhaps the most difficult area of systematic theology to treat from a feminist perspective within the Roman Catholic tradition' (337). This is so, because of, as she puts it, the Catholic Church's 'intractably patriarchal and hierarchal' traditions and structures, which cause many 'discouraged and alienated' women to move or to work outside the church.

New Testament scholar Elizabeth Schüssler Fiorenza presents the church as 'a discipleship of equals'; her critique of patriarchy has broadened to an admission that it involves not just gender, but also class and race, and that 'power differentials exist among women as well' (338). Elizabeth Johnson too writes of the church's need to become a 'community of mutuality among equal persons' and she highlights the notion of the

Communion of saints, with Mary understood as elder sister (and not so much as Mother) in this context. Anne Carr also argues for an egalitarian model of church, using the issue of women's ordination to make her point about contrasting ecclesiologies – those who oppose ordination have a notion of God or Christ as masculine and active in relation to the community as feminine and receptive (339), whereas those in favour stress the one priesthood of all believers through baptism. Rosemary Radford Ruether has written about Women-Church, stressing the need for women to express solidarity with one another and draw sustenance from this, a kind of exodus counter-cultural movement that is called to abandon the established social order. It is not enough to press for change in the church, she argues, one needs also 'bases for a feminist critical culture and celebrational community that have some autonomy from the established institutions' (340). Mary Hines praises Vatican II with its notion of *communio* and draws on Ruether and Schlüsser-Fiorenza, but also on Karl Rahner. You will know the voices of many Irish women in this debate – think of Pauline Logue Collins, Marie Collins, Mary Condren, Áilín Doyle, Bernadette Flanagan, Maureen Gaffney, Linda Hogan, Marie Keenan, Maureen Junker Kenny, Betty Maher, Mary Malone, President Mary McAleese,[11] Margaret MacCurtin, Gina Menzies, Cathy Molloy, Suzanne Mulligan, Breda O'Brien, Helena O'Donoghue, Nuala O'Loan, Ethna Regan, Fainche Ryan, Geraldine Smyth, Gesa Thiessen, Anne Thurston, Soline Vatinel, Katherine Zappone, and many, many others.

In summary, it would be untrue to say that nothing has

---

11. Besides many other contributions, it is interesting to note that Mary McAleese completed a research MA in Canon Law at the Milltown Institute in 2010, her thesis being on the subject of Collegiality in the Code of Canon Law. In her Valedictorian Address at the Conferring Ceremony on 20 October 2010 President McAleese pays tribute to 'that wise old man of Canon Law, the great Jesuit and theologian Ladislas Orsy, who has made the academic critique and development of collegiality and *communio* within the church his life's work' – Irish Jesuit AMDG web-site, Nov 9, 2010.

changed since the Second Vatican Council. In Ireland, in particular, we do have a much more participative church, with lay
people altogether more visible in terms of formal and informal
ministries such as readers, Eucharistic ministers, pastoral assist-
ants, and with the admittedly uneven development of parish
councils and so on. And of course, as I noted before, the enduring value of the church is evident on all kinds of special occasions like baptisms, weddings and funerals, while on a more ordinary level prayer-groups, daily and weekly eucharist, retreats,
theology courses and social outreach are enrichment for many,
both within and outside the church.

However, as the crisis in Ireland, the critique of Orsy and the
observations of the many voices just quoted indicate, progress
has been patchy and far too limited, while in many cases we
have witnessed regression.[12] Above all there has been a failure
to empower real co-responsibility, to allow a share in governance. Inspired by the vision of Vatican II we need to imagine a
new culture and structures which would allow for more effective participation and shared decision-making without, as Dulles
cautions, losing that unity which enables the church to offer
global leadership. We need to do this in an era when, provident-
ially, we are much more conscious than the fathers of Vatican II
of the equal dignity and role of women. Other 'signs of the
times' since Vatican II are the phenomena of globalisation,
helped by the extraordinary developments in communications
technology; the fall of communism and the spread of democracy,
albeit in a context of global terrorism; the raising of consciousness around environmental concerns; the continuing gap between rich and poor, not least in a context of the international
economic and financial recession; the new interest in inter-reli-

---

12. The irenic critique of Christopher O'Donnell, op cit, 461, made in
1996, is even more to the point since: 'In the post-Vatican II period there
has been a dialectic between the institutional view of the church and
the new openings from the council ... though neither has emerged as
victorious, it would seem that in some cases, there is greater weight
given to what were the concerns of the minority of the council rather
than to new beginnings supported by the will of the majority'.

gious dialogue, in particular the dialogue with Islam and its far-reaching political ramifications; and, of course, the terrible proximate cause of all our soul-searching, the scandal of child sexual abuse within the church.

Part Two: The Current Situation

4.1 Analysis
The fault-lines of our current ecclesial situation, in Ireland and worldwide, have been cruelly exposed by the scandal of clerical child sexual abuse (CSA) and its mishandling by church authorities. It remains an absolute priority that justice is done to survivors and victims and that safeguards are put in place to ensure that the church becomes an exemplary safe place for children. But it will be a tribute to survivors, rather than exploitation, if we can also avail of the *kairos* which their terrible fate has thrown up to carry out a more widespread reform of the church.

I have argued elsewhere[13] (as have many others, including Brendan Callaghan, Patrick Claffey, Eamon Conway, Donald Cozzens, Paul Dempsey, Donal Dorr, Bishop Kevin Dowling, Eamon Duffy, Eugene Duffy, Sean Freyne, Maureen Gaffney, Brendan Hoban, Marie Keenan, Nicholas Lash, Brian Lennon, Mary Malone, Archbishop Diarmuid Martin, Pádraig McCarthy, Enda McDonagh, Sean McDonagh, Michael McGuckian, Gina Menzies, Cathy Molloy, Suzanne Mulligan, Helena O'Donoghue, Nuala O'Loan, Kieran O'Mahony, Owen O'Sullivan, David Power, Timothy Radcliffe, Fainche Ryan, Thomas Whelan) that the CSA crisis has exposed a deeper crisis and even dysfunctionality in our church.[14] This dysfunctionality, in my view, emanates

13. O'Hanlon, articles in 2010 in *The Furrow/Studies*
14. I note in this context the Press Statement of 28 December 2010 from the Association of Catholic Priests, in response to the article by Bishop Freeman in *The Irish Times* of the same date, which says, *inter alia*, that '… if the response to the issue clerical child sexual abuse is not seen in the broader context of the "shortcomings in structure and function of the church", then it will be ultimately futile, and that a great opportunity will be lost'.

from a problematic nexus of issues around sexuality, power and the relationship between them.

There is, first, the simple fact that many good people do not find that church teaching on sexuality (for example, on contraception/divorce and remarriage/sexual orientation/gender and the role of women) is credible and so it does not nourish their intimate lives. It would be a mistake to imagine that this incredulity is limited to intellectuals or liberals too easily accommodated to contemporary culture. I would say, for example, that the felt treatment of women as second-class citizens within our church is widely shared, from Connemara to Dublin 4. I am reminded of the special pleading from Africa and Eastern Europe among Jesuits when a document on women in the church was being debated in 1995: in the event that said more about the social/cultural level of awareness in those parts of the world at the time than it did about the actual situation of women. We need urgently to address this situation of women in our church – the *status quo* is both untenable and unconscionable and, if not addressed, will leave the church as an enclave hospitable to traditionalists only. Our church ought to be catholic not just in the universal sense but also in the sense that it can value traditionalist, middle-of-the-road people, as well as intellectuals, some of whom may be liberal: it is patently not succeeding in this respect in these times.

There are excellent aspects to church teaching on sexuality (locating it in a personalist context, stressing commitment and fidelity, the value of exclusivity in marriage and so on), but it gets lost because of doctrinal positions and use of language which the faithful, for the most part, find untrue to human experience. This is a grave situation for a church which claims to base its moral teaching on the natural law, accessible to human reason. To call this teaching prophetic or counter-cultural in a positive sense, because in many respects it goes against what is generally accepted in contemporary culture, is to take a leap too far, unless at the same time one can show how the teaching is not unreasonable. One recalls the remarks of Cardinal Suenens at Vatican II in this context: 'We must avoid another Galileo case. One is enough for the church' (O'Malley, 238). There may come a point when, as the resigning spokesperson for the leader of the Church in Belgium, Archbishop Léonard, said, the constant repetition of unreceived, supposedly counter-cultural teaching, becomes a bit like driving against the oncoming traffic, stubbornly maintaining that everyone else is wrong.[15] If the teaching is unreasonable then the moral authority of the church is severely dented – the intimate life of men and women is central to who they are and it is a huge let-down if they experience failure in guidance from the church in this area.

This failure is compounded by the lack of discussion surrounding the formulation and reception of this teaching. The 'don't ask, don't tell' culture that the Murphy Report (1, 31) criticises with regard to the handling of CSA has much wider and deeper ramifications in our church. In lots of overt ways (the express prohibition of advocacy of the ordination of women) and ways that are more subtle (criteria for the appointment of bishops, withdrawal of licence to teach in Catholic institutions, blocks to promotion) our church adopts a culture of 'don't ask, don't tell', of secrecy, fear and deference in relation to disputed theological issues, in particular in relation to sexuality and gender. The recent ecclesiastical reprimand of Irish Capuchin Owen O'Sullivan is a case in point. This culture is then reinforced by the type of centralised authority structures, without sufficient checks and balances at intermediate and peripheral levels, which we have noted permeates the organisation of the Catholic Church and which Vatican II tried to remedy. And so, when Bishop Willie Walsh on several occasions voiced concern over some of these disputed areas of Catholic morality, arguably he was doing exactly what, in the theory of Vatican II's understanding of the autonomous role of a bishop in his diocese – consulting the 'sense of the faithful' in the laity – a bishop should

---

15. 'Archbishop Léonard has sometimes acted like someone who's driving against the traffic and thinks everyone else is in the wrong' – Jürgen Mettepenningen, former spokesman for the Archbishop, *Irish Times*, Tuesday, 9 November 2010

do. But, as the great silence from fellow bishops and the calls to Rome made clear, he was not behaving according to the operative self-understanding of the church.

4.2 The Church as Organisation

Can we get any help from the insights and observations of organisational, structural and cultural theorists in imagining more concretely the shape of a church which might be true to the insights of Vatican II and responsive to the needs of our times?

Systemic psychotherapist Dr Marie Keenan, with considerable experience in dealing with victims and perpetrators of clerical child sexual abuse, writes from an organisational cultural perspective.[16] She describes the church as a 'closed' organisation in the sense of its clerics being individuals trying to meet their personal, professional, social and sexual needs inside the boundary of the one organisation – in such an organisation, according to the research literature, if there is not active listening to those it purports to serve, there is more likely to be high risk in terms of sexual, physical or mental exploitation, the risk being higher if and when the leadership is centralised and not accountable and when there are insufficient checks and balances in the exercise of power and control (7-8). Also (9) there can be in organisations a type of routine nonconformity to the institution's own formal goals and standards, which then becomes a type of institutional conformity (so, for example, the non-reporting of crime to civil authorities, the failure to insist on conditions of communication and consultation necessary for any effective exercise of shared responsibility and so on). And so, as Keenan puts it, it will not do simply to have better screening of candidates if the heart of the problem is not so much individual deviance as conformity with the mistaken contours of an organisation which needs reform: 'It has been long established by social scientists and theologians that a review of the church's governance structures, power-relations and sexual ethics are long overdue. In light

16. Dr Marie Keenan, 'An Organizational Cultural Perspective on Child Sexual Abuse in the Catholic Church', *Doctrine and Life*, 60, October 2010, 4-14

of the sexual abuse crisis change is now even more pertinent. Despite the various wake-up calls, the current line from Rome makes clear that these topics must remain untouched' (12).

In similar vein, organisational psychologist Sean Ruth notes how groups with a high level of cohesion and positive self-regard, but also groups with a culture of fear and conformity, were more likely to entertain a form of 'groupthink' which, despite the intelligence and well-meaning morality of the individuals concerned, led to dysfunctional decision making.[17] All this is reinforced when we add power and an insulation from outside or opposing views to a culture that already encourage groupthink (103-5). In this context it becomes very important to change the system, not just the actors within the system. Ruth goes on to characterise the culture of the Roman Catholic Church in Ireland as, among other things, distant, secretive, conforming, defensive and hierarchical. He notes that those in leadership are male and clerical – also they are older, celibate, middle-class and white. Their role is to instruct, guide, challenge a hugely diverse church population that includes women, young people, victims of abuse, people of colour, lay men and women, working-class people, religious – to name but a few. In this context, without in any way judging the motives, intentions or goodness of these church leaders ('nice people'), it is no wonder 'that the leadership of the church is simply out of touch with the feelings, the thinking, and the experiences of many of these groups' (106-7). Ruth goes on to note that there is a principle about leadership that says it is not possible to do the thinking for people. What is possible is to think with them. To do this effectively and to be able to think clearly about any situation, requires a leader to listen to the people (108). Where there is good leadership the leaders rely less and less on the trappings of authority. Where this is not so leaders 'insist on the right to command, to decide things unilaterally, to be obeyed, to be treated

---

17. Sean Ruth, 'Responding to Abuse: Culture, Leadership and Change', in John Littleton and Eamon Maher, eds, *The Dublin/Murphy Report: A Watershed in Irish Catholicism?*, Dublin: Columba, 2010, 102-112

with deference … in effect authority without leadership becomes authoritarian. In order to avoid this happening, authority has to embody leadership and … this entails active listening. The challenge for church leaders now is to move from occupying positions of authority to building those influence (sic) relationships' (109), to engage in a deep listening process with all the constituents of the church (110). Ruth concludes by saying that 'such a listening process could take place in a series of parish, diocesan and national assemblies or synods' (110).

The observations of prominent lay-woman Nuala O'Loan are pertinent in this context.[18] Drawing on her own experience as Police Ombudsman in Northern Ireland (1997-2007) O'Loan accepts the validity of the question *quis custodiet ipsos custodes?* (Who will guard the guards themselves?) in relation to her own exercise of power in the North and, by implication, to the exercise of power in the Catholic Church. This is a church which, albeit immensely powerful, ironically 'has long and, I think proudly, proclaimed that is is not a democracy' (267). Furthermore, O'Loan observes somewhat laconically: '… For the most part, there is no place for women in the governance of our church' (267). She answered the question in her own domain by ensuring that there were many layers of accountability and transparency in her exercise of power, and argues for some of the same safeguards within the church, analogous to the new safeguards around child sexual abuse which 'are a model for accountability' (270). O'Loan recommends a diocesan strategy which 'would require relevant training and norms for the delivery of services in a parish, which would require the existence of specific organisations, such as a properly empowered and functioning pastoral council, a diocesan pastoral council and a diocesan complaints mechanism, funded by the church and staffed by both clergy and laity, with a right of appeal to a national body … each parish, each diocese and each institution within the church could produce an annual report in an agreed format for the people.

---

18. Nuala O'Loan, 'Transparency, accountability and the exercise of power in the Church of the future', *Studies*, 99, Autumn, 2010, 267-275

Annual or bi-annual diocesan synods could be established to feed into national synods every three years or so, giving people a greater role in the life of the church' (270-271). O'Loan argues that this notion of accountability and transparency must be extended to include appropriate reform of Canon Law – 'canon law is fundamental to the operation of justice in the church, and justice must be seen to be done, and must be accessible' (272) – and to all matters financial.[19] She notes that a viable communications strategy is necessary to ensure a far greater understanding of the accountable and transparent church for which she argues (273-4).

Finally, in this context, I note the observations of Jesuit clinical psychologist Brendan Callaghan who, in common with so many others, notes[20] that the scandal of clerical child sexual abuse has revealed a defensive institutional culture in our church with which we have struggled for over five centuries (347). The church of the first half of the twentieth century, he adds, was one where authoritarianism and defensiveness fed each other (348). And, despite the shift in consciousness of Vatican II, there are still too many dysfunctional aspects to the exercise of power within the church. Callaghan cites studies which indicate the characteristics of functional and dysfunctional groups and it may be helpful to list some of these: no talk rule/open communication; internalised feelings/expressed feelings; unspoken expectations/explicit rules; entangled relationships/respect for individuation; manipulation and control/respect for freedom; chaotic value system/consistent value system; rigid attitudes/

19. In this context it is worth citing again the *Motu Proprio data* of Pope Benedict XVI on 30 December 2010 in which the Vatican, whose bank is the focus of a money laundering investigation within Italy, has enacted laws to bring it in line with international standards on financial transparency and the fight against funding terrorism. In an accompanying Press Release Vatican spokesman Federico Lombardi locates this move in the context of the transparency, honesty and responsibility spoken about in the encyclical *Caritas in Veritate* (2009, n 36) and finishes his statement by saying: 'This is a good way to conclude the year: with a step towards transparency and credibility'. Well, quite – and hopefully the many other steps needed, on so many other fronts, may soon follow!
20. Brendan Callaghan, 'On Scandal and scandals: the psychology of clerical paedophilia', *Studies*, 99, Autumn, 2010, 343-356

open mindedness; reveres past tradition/creates new tradition; dependent relationships/independence and growth; jealousy and suspicion/trust and love. Of course not all the dysfunctional qualities listed in the first part of each couplet apply to all aspects of the church, 'but it can be argued that sufficient of them apply sufficiently for us to have real concern' (349-350). Callaghan goes on to describe this culture in terms of a clericalism which encouraged secrecy but which also relied on the collusion and corresponsibility of all of us: 'For any culture to endure within an institution, a large proportion of the members of the institution have to support it, explicitly or implicitly, actively or passively. That a clericalist culture has survived within the church is a shared responsibility of us all' (350). The 'gains' for clergy in this culture included status/privilege, power, lack of accountability, and freedom from relational commitments and responsibilities; the 'gains' for laity included the avoidance of responsibility, a clearly defined role, the avoidance of the costs of adult faith, and the security and 'reflected glory' that derive from dependence on another (351). Callaghan ends his piece with a reflection on the paschal mystery of death and resurrection and while he notes that there is no place for a calculus of horror weighing the tragic cost of abuse against what can emerge by way of a renewed church, still he hopes that 'out of the wreck of a defensive, conformist, clerical culture, a new pattern of being church is emerging' (354).

The CSA scandal has given bishops, and us all, an opportunity to realise that this culture of fear and excessive deference is neither true to the gospel, as articulated by Vatican II, nor is it adequate to address the crisis that we are in and the many people who suffer greatly because of it. These include the survivors of CSA, and also the many others, including women who, in the words of a parish newsletter,[21] 'find themselves in a strained re-

---

21. Taken from the Naas, Sallins, Two Mile House newsletter, 26 September, 2010 advertising a Silent Walk of Solidarity with the survivors and victims of CSA but also with those 'who find themselves in a strained relationship with the institutional church because of gender issues, sexual orientation or relationship situations'.

lationship with the institutional church'. They also include those who have already left the church, or those altogether outside the church but who have a right – if our own language of being a 'light to the world' is to be believed – to responsible witness from us Catholics. In the light of what we have learned about the dangers of not challenging the prevailing culture (Bishop Jim Moriarty), there is a real call now to our bishops in Ireland to step up to the mark in a responsible, adult way and not simply operate exclusively out of the default position that Rome is always right, even if the people before me in my diocese are not at peace. And similarly we all – lay faithful, priests, religious, bishops – need to ask for the kind of conversion which will allow us to be assertive in the responsible and prudent way that is adult. I say conversion, because it is not easy to change from unquestioning deference to critical respect: this is a change in the habits of a lifetime, and it will bear fruit (like Gamaliel says, in Acts 5:38-39) if it comes not just from human striving but from a heart and mind filled with God's love. The words of Orsy are apt in this context. He notes that 'if the papacy ought to change, so must the faithful' (11), and then in a footnote he gives some examples – 'the bishops who shun personal decisions and turn to Rome for guidance, *opportune et importune* (in season and out of season), contribute as much to centralisation as any Roman office can. Theologians who exalt the personal theological opinions of the pope into Catholic doctrine (which he never intended) are destroying intellectual diversity in the church. The faithful who distort the respect due to 'sacred pastors' (cf Canon 212) into a cult of personality are hurting Christ's body – the church' (Orsy, 11-12).

4.3 The Key issue: the balance between primacy and collegiality

Before going on to outline some possible ways forward I want to discuss further the key issue which emerges from our discussion so far.

I refer to the absolutely central issue of how to understand more clearly the relationship between primacy (Vatican I) and collegiality (Vatican II). We have noted how Vatican II corrected the one-sidedness of Vatican I by balancing primacy with collegiality: yet for the most part the two principles were simply asserted side by side and 'consensus was not generally achieved by a higher viewpoint which would take up in a richer unity the diverse viewpoints'.[22] O'Donnell (461) hints that the resolution may already be apparent in Vatican II, since the Holy Spirit is the principle of both communion and hierarchy (*LG* 4:10-11). But this will remain a rather formal solution unless it is rooted in some clearer teaching and, above all, institutional change which leads to structures effecting an operative 'unity in diversity' with regard to leadership. Otherwise, as we have seen, the sheer weight of the statements of Vatican I, no matter how carefully nuanced, tend towards the interpretation of Bismarck (bishops as instruments of the pope) and primacy always trumps collegiality, as has happened.

I would caution against what Balthasar has called an 'anti-Roman affect' as we struggle to resolve this issue. If the church is to be truly a world church it needs strong central leadership (not least, of course, to counteract clerical child sexual abuse where, it may be supposed, there is still much denial and resistance in many parts of the Catholic world). It is a great gift from God to have such a normative service of unity and love in the papacy (Eamon Duffy, Avery Dulles); we should not idealise the conciliar and synodal procedures of other Christian communions (Orthodox, Eastern Catholics, Anglican, Presbyterians and so on) as if they presented us with some ready-made solution. Often they too will admit to a felt need for some more decisive word from the centre – witness, for example, the terrible struggles of Anglicanism in these times to preserve their rich diversity in some kind of meaningful unity.[23] Besides, we should recognise that however authority is exercised we human

---

22. C. O'Donnell, op cit, 460; Fahey, op cit, 381

23. In this context the struggles of Rowan Williams, Archbishop of Canterbury, are outlined graphically in the biography by Rupert Shortt, *Rowan's Rule*, London: Hodder and Stoughton, 2008. However, one notes also the characteristically admirable and lucid ongoing, committed engagement of Rowan Williams with the substantive issues raised by *Ut*

beings often find it difficult to reconcile our desire for autonomy with obedience to the common good – Dulles is right to observe that there is a good deal of quarrelling within Orthodoxy; it happens within Protestantism as well, and we should not imagine that there is a strife-free way forward. And, as has been mentioned, the search for an ideal form of leadership and government is familiar also in the secular sphere, as institutions, countries and continents like the United Nations, the United States of American and the European Union, to name but a few, illustrate.

Nonetheless, with all these caveats in mind, we do well to seek a 'better balance' and to note that we can learn a lot from political scientists, theorists of social organisation, the successes and failures of different forms of secular government as we search for a better way forward for the church. Above all we should desist from sweeping declarations that of course 'the church is not a democracy', as if there is not abundant evidence to show that the church has always had many democratic elements in its make-up, and as if we could so easily recommend democracy to the secular world in Catholic Social Teaching and then pretend to reject its relevance for our own ecclesial polity.

It is indeed quite ironic and bizarre in the extreme that, according to Richard McBrien, 'there are only two places in the entire corpus of Catholic social teaching where the teachings on social justice and human rights are explicitly applied to the church itself'.[24] McBrien goes on to note that Pius XII in a Christmas address in 1946 did make the obvious connection of

---

Unum Sint, expressed yet again at a recent address given at the Vatican as part of a conference to commemorate the fiftieth anniversary of the Pontifical Council for Promoting Christian Unity: '... the agenda of *Ut Unum Sint* must not be allowed to slip out of sight ... there are many historic sensitivities about the cultural expression of the petrine ministry and indeed about the theological expressions of its authority in the modern period ... but these should not be allowed to obscure the need to clarify what is the service that can and should be given to an apostolic church by the petrine ministry' – *The Tablet Speeches*, 13 December, 2010

24. McBrien, op cit, 254 – the two instances cited are the document *Iustitia in Mundo* (Justice in the World), chapter 3, from the Synod Bishops 1971 and the U.S Catholic Bishops' pastoral letter *Economic Justice for All*, n 347, 1986

applying the 1931 teaching of Pius XI on subsidiarity to the church itself and that the Revised Code of Canon Law (1983) makes the same connection: 'Careful attention is to be given to the greater application of the so-called principle of subsidiarity within the church. It is a principle which is rooted in a higher one because the office of bishops with its attached powers is a reality of divine law' (n 5 – McBrien, 255). Bishop Kevin Dowling is trenchant in his critique of church praxis in this respect, noting that '... if church leadership anywhere presumes to criticise or critique socio-political-economic policies and policy makers, or governments, it must allow itself to be critiqued in the same way in terms of its policies, its internal life, and especially its *modus operandi*', and goes on to assert that '... today we have a leadership in the church which actually undermines the very notion of subsidiarity'.[25] In similar vein James Corkery, writing about the pontificate of John Paul II, notes the concern about a dissonance between the pope's *ad extra* and *ad intra* pronouncements and behaviour.[26]

In this context the complement to Balthasar's warnings about an 'anti-Roman affect' is his earlier slogan about the advisability of 'razing the ramparts' – the church needs to discern between positive and negative aspects of secularisation and to humbly admit that it can learn from as well as teach 'the world'. If it can do this in relation to the Vatican Bank by enacting laws to ensure greater transparency (see note 19 above), why not also apply the other values and principle of Catholic Social Teaching in a more rigorous and explicit way to the organisational structure and culture of the church?

25. Bishop Kevin Dowling, 'The Current State of the Church', *The Furrow*, 61, November 2010, 591-597 at 594-5

26. Corkery, op cit, refers to the critique by Hans Küng that the pope 'had supported human rights *ad extra* but had withheld them *ad intra* – from bishops, theologians, and women, above all ... he had blocked reform within the church, refused dialogue, and set as his goal absolute Roman rule' (239); and to the observation by Gerard Mannion that perhaps the pope's own experience of totalitarian regimes, of rebellion *ad extra* and unity *ad intra* might be related to his demands for unswerving allegiance from theologians (240).

As noted by Orsy at the beginning of this book, what we are looking for is a better balance, a need which the pope himself recognised in his 1995 appeal. There is of course an honourable tradition within Catholic theology of critical questioning of magisterial statements – Joseph Ratzinger, for example, wrote in 1969 about the ground on which even radical criticism of papal doctrinal statements could be based: 'Criticism of papal pronouncements will be possible and even necessary, to the degree that they lack support in scripture and creed, that is, in the faith of the whole church. When neither the consensus of the whole church is had, nor clear evidence from the sources is available, a definitive decision is not possible. Were one formally to take place, while conditions for such were lacking, the question would have to be raised concerning its legitimacy.'[27] One recalls too the understanding of Newman about how the lay faithful had preserved the truths of Nicea in the face of episcopal opposition, and his belief that 'the church was healthiest when able to encourage people to an intelligent grasp of their faith'.[28] So, while, from a Catholic point of view, it would be naïve and a form of Utopian fuzziness to imagine that persuasion and good example on their own will be enough to win assent always to disputed teaching, while the authority of office will be necessary to hold together the many disparate views and opinions and to challenge the recalcitrant and often narcissistic human spirit, still appeal to reason and the 'sense of the faithful' remain important dimensions of any authoritative ecclesial teaching, dimensions that are too often lacking in the Catholic Church since the First Vatican Council.

Ratzinger's strong statement about the freedom to offer a critique in the ambit of doctrine and the non-faith presuppositions of dogmatic statements is analogous to Karl Rahner's notion that the church's understanding of the supreme and permanent power of jurisdiction of the pope over the whole church and its

27. In Francis A. Sullivan SJ, *Magisterium*, Dublin: Gill and Macmillan, 1985, 208-209
28. Mansfield, op cit, 127

demarcation with the legitimate autonomy of intermediate bodies and persons is not a matter to be decided by the pope alone –
'For it cannot be claimed that the concrete and changeable settle-
ment of this demarcation is simply dependent on a decision of
the pope, not rationally to be justified and not open to appeal,
solely because the pope is not subject to any higher earthly decision-making authority in the church ... this demarcation ... can
certainly be decided by objective arguments, even if the latter
also take into account the pope's understanding of the issue ...
all general norms of Christian morality and of a system of law
understood in a truly Christian sense ... are genuinely valid and
should be applied without hesitation' (Rahner,119).

However these real, true, nuanced expressions of the limitations inherent in papal primacy have failed in large part, as
noted, to halt the seemingly inexorable centralisation within our
church. And this centralisation has, as argued, led to the kind of
deafness to the voice of ordinary Catholics, to that kind of
'closed' organisation spoken of by sociologists, in which 'repressed truth becomes poisonous' (Maximos), in which Acton's
dictum about the corruption of absolute power can too easily be
verified. And so, whereas the vision of Vatican II is attractive, it
needs further clarification. The judgement of Fahey is apposite
in this respect: '... it is regrettable that the Second Vatican
Council lacked the resoluteness to reformulate in a more satis-
factory way many of the obscure expressions of the First Vatican
Council. For instance, the First Vatican Council did not indicate
the limitations to papal primacy, and so one might conclude that
none exists. Clearly, however, the *plenitudo potestatis* has its limits in the will of Christ's institution of the church. Perhaps the
fact that the Second Vatican Council did not give non-Catholic
observers voice to raise questions from the floor of the council
meant that clarification could not come from that setting, but
could come initially only from bilateral consensus statements'
(Fahey, 382).

Among such bilateral, ecumenical statements is ARCIC II
(1999), already referred to, which breathes an altogether differ-

ent air in its treatment of primacy and infallibility. It speaks of 'a universal primacy, exercised collegially in the context of synodality, as integral to *episcope* as the service of universal communion; such a primacy having always been associated with the Bishop and the See of Rome' (pars 46-48). It goes on to speak in terms of the ministry of the Bishop of Rome as assisting 'the ministry of the whole episcopal body in the context of synodality, promoting the communion of the local churches in their life of Christ and the proclamation of the gospel' (par 46-48). It speaks of the 'essential co-operation of the ministry of *episcope* and the *sensus fidei* of the whole church in the reception of the Word of God' (pars 29, 36, and 43). Indeed this same notion of respect for diversity without threat to unity is already present within the Eastern Catholic Church, as the recent Synod of Bishops for the Middle East illustrated so well. Participants in this Synod noted that the Eastern Catholic Churches, while in full communion with the pope, have their own canon law and disciplines, their own liturgies, spiritualities, histories and heritage; they have married clergy; and they have a vision of church 'as a network where unity does not mean uniformity and where communion grows through communication and sharing' (October 12, 2010, Catholic News Service).

I am proposing then that we need further precision on the teaching of Vatican II on the relationship between primacy and collegiality (which may well require a further Ecumenical Council). Above all, since teaching often follows action, we need the structural/institutional expressions of collegiality which Vatican II failed to provide and which will involve a more collegial government of the whole church from Rome (see Maximos) and a reform of the Roman Curia in ways which make it administrative rather than executive in function. Nicholas Lash writes in the spirit of Maximos and in direct allusion to Archbishop Quinn: 'What we need, and what (in my judgement) it is not unrealistic to hope for, is the election of a pope who, broadly sharing Archbishop's Quinn diagnosis of the problem, establishes a commission, which the pope would chair, whose members would be perhaps 40 or 50 diocesan bishops, drawn from every corner of the world, and which would be advised by officials of the Roman Curia, and by historians, theologians and canon lawyers from outside Rome (many of whom, of course, might by laypeople, women as well as men). The task of this commission would be to draw up proposals for the transfer of governance in the church from pope and Curia to pope and bishops, through the establishment of a standing synod whose members would be diocesan bishops and whose work would be assisted by the offices of a Curia so reformed as to function, not as an instrument of governance, but as a service of administration. The work of this commission, when completed, would then be submitted to the worldwide episcopate for comment, and, presumably revision, before receiving from the pope its final ratification. The centralised control from which we suffer, and which has contributed so greatly to the present crisis of authority, was built up in less than 100 years. It could be put into reverse in less than ten.'[29]

I simply note, in brief, a sub-set of this important issue to which previous reference has also been made. It often seems in discussions of this kind that doctrine, and especially dogma, instead of being liberating (Flannery O'Connor speaks of dogma as 'the guardian of mystery' – M. P. Gallagher, 82) become a form of imprisonment which hinder the response to real need and the pastoral situation of our time (criteria which, you recall, where at the heart of the development of the early church). But 'the word of God is not fettered' (2 Tim 2:9) – there is a lively debate going on in our church about the notion of development of doctrine, so implicit in the process of Vatican II and so dear to the hearts of theologians like Newman and Lonergan. Is this development understandable only in terms of a 'hermeneutic of continuity', or do we not also find that there is real discontinuity also? And if, as Lonergan contends, discontinuity may be understood in terms of the essential role of dialectic in the emer-

---

29. N. Lash, *Theology for Pilgrims*, London: Darton, Longman and Todd, 2008, 239

gence of truth, as well as in terms of various differentiations of consciousness, still, if this applies to reformable doctrine only and not to dogma, how does it help in the revision of the dogmatic teaching of Vatican I?

Interestingly Michael Fahey (391-2) notes that while commonly in the West we speak of 20 ecumenical councils (among them Vatican I and II), this number has never been dogmatically defined and Paul VI expressed the conviction that there are two sorts of councils in the patrimony of the West, the early ecumenical councils of the undivided church and then the later general synods of the West. So, in 1974 Paul IV referred to the Second Council of Lyons (traditionally part of the list of 20) as 'the sixth of the general synods held in the West' (392). Fahey observes that this terminology of 'general synods' suggests 'that Catholic teaching is willing to accept the notion of varying levels of councils, what Yves Congar has called a hierarchy or relative order of importance among councils and synods (*hierarchia conciliorum*)'. It is unlikely that this approach on its own can explain away the dogmatic force for Catholics of Vatican I: it is more likely, as has been the case with disputed questions from Trent, that the passing of time, the new pressure of events, ecumenical dialogue with non-Catholics which includes this notion of a 'hierarchy of councils', attention to our needs now in this pastoral situation and the 'sense of the faithful' as both source and receptive criterion[30] of authentic ecclesial teaching will be used by the Holy Spirit to effect a new resolution.

I note finally, on a related issue, that a pastoral letter of the German bishops from 22 September 1967,[31] often quoted by Karl Rahner, recognises that in its effort to apply the gospel to the changing situations of life the church is obliged to give instructions that have certain provisionality about them. These in-

---

30. For an interesting discussion on significance of the mixed reception to church teaching on sex and war, see Linda Hogan, 'Mixed Reception: Paul VI and John Paul II on sex and war', in Corkery and Worcester, op cit, 2010, 204-222

31. Quoted and discussed in Sullivan, 1983, 156-158 and A. Dulles, 'Authority and Conscience', *Church*, Autumn 1986, 9-10

structions, though binding to a certain degree, are subject to error and dissent, may be legitimate provided it is responsible. The letter is realistic in recognising that in life in general we cannot expect certainty in all matters – 'every doctor in his diagnosis, every statesman in the political judgements he arrives at on particular situations and the decisions he bases on these, is aware of this fact' (Sullivan, 156). But even if this is so, '... the church ... in her doctrine and practice cannot always and in every case allow herself to be caught in the dilemma of either arriving at a doctrinal decision which is ultimately binding or simply being silent and leaving everything to the free opinion of the individual ... otherwise it would be quite impossible for her to preach or to interpret her faith as a decisive force in real life or to apply it to each new situation in human life as it arises' (157). This is a liberating kind of approach which effectively counters any tendency to that 'creeping infallibility' we have noted in response to even the ordinary papal magisterium. It is not, however, an approach which is widespread today in the Catholic Church.

CHAPTER FIVE

A Way Forward – 7 Theses

The battle for the Promised Land waged and '... As long as Moses kept his arms raised, Israel has the advantage ... But Moses' arms grew heavy, so they took a stone and put it under him and on this he sat, Aaron and Hur supporting his arms, one on one side, one on the other; and his arms remained firm till sunset' (Exodus 17:11-12)

Not all will agree with all details of the analysis presented in the preceding four chapters, but many will agree with much of it and most will agree that our situation is grave. In this context we need a conversation, a listening and talking, to come up with an agreed way forward. My proposals here are intended as a contribution to this process: it is much too early to present a cut and dried blue print, but neither must we allow complexity to paralyse us.

We may anticipate much resistance: human beings are normally afraid of change, an institution as venerable and well-defended as the church has long experience of how to maintain the *status quo* and, besides, there are no easy solutions to the relationship between primacy and collegiality at all its many levels (even if we have more than enough pointers in ecclesial and secular spheres to permit us to take responsible initiatives). The temptation to 'ride out the crisis' will be great, not least because everywhere we are surrounded by truly good, 'nice' people who will hope that with a bit of tinkering, better management and communications strategy, the current basic model of church may survive. We need to resist this temptation and use the crisis as an opportunity to imagine something different, new, more faithful to Vatican II and to the New Testament. We have a serious obligation 'not to stifle the Spirit' (1 Thess 5:19). In this spirit I offer the following seven ways forward (not quite on a par with Luther's 95 theses, for which the patient reader may indeed be grateful!

1. *'As long as Moses kept his arms raised...' – the centrality of prayer*
Our baptism, our being in the church, is a call and gift from God. We are also creatures of our own times, times when secularism has made deep inroads into our imagination and consciousness. In this context we easily tend to forms of Gnosticism, Donatism and Pelagianism, to imagine that reformation depends primarily on our own efforts and that it implies a rigorism and perfection-ism that are elitist and uncharacteristic of the church of saints and sinners called by Jesus Christ. The Good News of Jesus Christ, the glorious freedom of the sons and daughters of God, are gifts of the Holy Spirit and it is in response to these gifts that we go forward. One thinks again of the Gamaliel principle: if this is from God it will succeed (Acts 5:38-39). And so we need to find ways of building prayer into our communal discernment, of asking for the kind of freedom that prayer gives, the kind of freedom that can acknowledge the goodness of other people and yet can firmly assert opposing truths, that can rest at peace with the 'already, not yet' eschatological proviso which is intrinsic to the coming of God's kingdom in history.

Sometimes prayer is used as a substitute for action or as a kind of softening of the brain and mollifying of the spirit that leads to blandness. But this was not the prayer of Moses (during the battle, in Exodus 17), not the prayer of Jesus (his opposition to the Scribes and Pharisees, the money-lenders in the Temple), not the prayer of Ignatius of Loyola nor of the rest of the saints. Rather, I am speaking of the type of prayer that leads to decision (discernment) and motivates action, that keeps us going over the long haul, through that 'long march' through the institutions that can be so painful that it really is a paschal experience, in-volving cross and resurrection.

In many of the issues we have mentioned, without prayer we will simply not get started at all or quickly give up, such are the difficulties involved. So, for example, how is a woman, sensitive to her status within our church, to take on this battle when there seems so little hope of progress? In this, and in many other issues, we have all heard phrases like 'they'll never change' many times over the past few years as the church has seemed to blunder from crisis to crisis with little sign of learning. Do we imagine that Jesus had it easy, do we not recall the grumbling of the people on the march to the Promised Land, do we not remember that Abraham was asked to 'hope against hope', do we think it will be different for us? We need as church to root ourselves deeply in the soil of a dynamic, action-oriented prayer and spirituality – and the pope was right about this in his letter to us, and this is precisely where places like the Jesuit Retreat Centre Manresa (location of the series of talks which were at the origin of this book) and the many other centres of spirituality in Ireland can offer resources to all of us at this difficult but hopeful time.

2. *The voice of the lay faithful needs to be heard*

I remember in the 34th General Congregation of the Society of Jesus, which I attended in 1995, we issued a decree on the laity which, *inter alia*, described the church of the new millennium as the church of the laity.[1] Around that time too there was a lot of talk around the notion of 'creative fidelity'[2] – a sense of wanting to be loyal to the church, but recognising that sometimes, often, this loyalty required the kind of creativity which could ruffle feathers. I have tried to sketch a context in which the role of the faithful, according to Vatican II, is primary, and yet is located within a polity which gives due respect to ordained leadership. And so, as Orsy put it, 'we are at a groundbreaking stage ... we ought to formulate our questions with utmost care' (12). I am not advocating a reactive rejection of all authority: quite simply, this

---

1. Decree 13, *Co-operation with the Laity in Mission*, par 1 of *Decrees of General Congregation 34 of Society of Jesus*, 1995
2. I note, in this context, the publication by Francis A. Sullivan SJ, *Creative Fidelity, Weighing and Interpreting Documents of the Magisterium*, Dublin: Gill and Macmillan, 1996

would no longer be the Catholic Church. But what I do think is required is for more and more lay people to speak up with the kind of responsible freedom which represents the *sensus fidelium* so treasured in conciliar documents and to claim that consultative and deliberative role in decision-making that is consonant with the letter and spirit of Vatican II. It seems to me that the momentum is with laity in these days: it will be laity who will exercise the kind of moral leadership which will get things moving.

Within laity I want to refer in particular to the voice of women. This is surely an unmistakable 'sign of the times', to which the church is arriving 'a little breathless and a little late' (well, very late, to be honest!). How can creative and faithful ways be found to honour the role of women in our church?[3]

There will be many suggestions as to how to mobilise the voice of the faithful in Ireland, including those of young people. I note that this is already happening – parish councils, parish assemblies, the Naas march, the creation in Dublin, Armagh, Down and Connor, Kerry and elsewhere of diocesan structures in which laity participate, the 'structured dialogue' initiative of Cardinal Brady and the Bishops' Council for Pastoral Renewal and Adult Faith Development in response to the papal letter to Irish Catholics[4] and supported by the Association of Catholic Priests,[5] and much more. It seems to me that all this could be

---

3. One notes that popes were not always elected by cardinals and that, more to our point, cardinals were not always in Holy Orders but also included lay people – hence the creative suggestion that perhaps the church should consider the option of women cardinals. Sometimes suggestions like this are regarded as 'cheap shots' and it is true that the implications (of non-episcopal cardinals, for one) would need to be thought through. But they do have a more serious and constructive 'shock value' in that they help to uncover false blocks in an establishment commonsense that surely has an admixture of nonsense, to use Lonergan's phrase. In this way they may help also to release our imaginations towards something more wholesome and sane.

4. Bishop Freeman, 'Rite and Reason', *The Irish Times*, 28 December 2010

5. See Statement of 28 December 2010, reported in *The Irish Times*, Wednesday 29 December 2010, which also says that 'the time may well be right for some form of assembly or synod of the church in Ireland'.

helped if some kind of data base could be built up of what is happening (including the use of contemporary social communications media like Facebook and Twitter, for which young people often have a particular facility). There are many skilled facilitators and processes designed to help groups conduct meetings in a safe space: I note, for example, the Omega process run by Mary Redmond and Una Henry and used in Balyboden and elsewhere to help parishes conduct open meetings in a constructive way.[6] All this will take time, and it will be messy: we need to re-invent those corporate habits of conversations, familiar to other churches, which centuries of clericalism have deleted from our corporate memories.

In time – and it need not be such a long time – we will identify the need to tackle systemic blocks (What, for example, happens when a sympathetic parish priest is changed and the new man doesn't allow meetings? Is canon 129 going to prevent a real share in decision-making?) and the need for a wider exchange at diocesan and national levels.

3. Bishops need to exercise real leadership

Both the Hebrew and Christian scriptures are graphic in their excoriating condemnation of religious leadership which is derelict in its duty – the bad shepherds (Ezekiel 34), the Scribes and Pharisees, blind leaders, hypocrites laying burdens on people (Mt 23). Our own leaders have gone through a most difficult time, with reprimands not just from media and general public, from church faithful, but also from the pope. Yet they are good men, trapped in a culture which has outlived its time.[7] And now, given all that has happened, given the responsibility to 'challenge the prevailing culture', they have a real opportunity of a redemptive change of style. This, I suggest, should occur on three main fronts.

First, they ought not to confuse 'strong leadership' with

6. Mary Redmond, 'Omega: The People's Voice – Reflections on Parish Consultation', *The Furrow*, 62, February 2011, 73-78

7. For a fuller analysis see O'Hanlon, *The Furrow*, 61, December 2010, 655-666

making decisions on their own: the Sacrament of Orders does give them a particular leadership role – and this must remain – but arguably what is most required of strong episcopal leadership today is precisely to empower the voice and effective participation of the laity. Secondly they need to act as a group with more common purpose (see below, n 4). And thirdly they need to take on a more adult, assertive role *vis-à-vis* the Holy See, to 'own' their own diocesan responsibilities, to articulate the 'sense of the faithful' and not simply have recourse to Rome for solutions to every question. The culture of deference has been revealed, in the CSA scandal, to be an enemy of the gospel. It is time now for our bishops to turn their backs on this culture, not just with respect to CSA but in all their dealings, including with Rome. They owe this to us, the church. The Apostolic Visitation offers a real opportunity for this different style of leadership: it should be used by Irish bishops in an open way to accept well-grounded criticism but also to articulate their own difficulties with how Rome has handled matters. Bishops should no longer use the default mechanism of 'peace with Rome' as an excuse for failing to listen to and articulate – in public and to Rome – the real concerns of the faithful in their dioceses. The practice of Willie Walsh in this respect should become the norm rather than the exception – remember the phrase of Maximos, 'repressed truths turn poisonous'.

Several recent interventions by Irish bishops in this context are worth noting – Bishop John Kirby of Clonfert, in a little-publicised contribution, said that among the topics discussed with the pope on the occasion of the infamous February 2010 meeting between Pope Benedict and the Irish bishops were 'a new understanding of sexuality and the role of women in the church', while he personally spoke to the pope about 'the responsibility of the church in Rome. The obligation of secrecy, originally promoted for the best of reasons, led to a culture of cover-up. The necessity to involve our own Irish state and report criminal activities was not emphasised. The failure to reply to correspondence gave a very bad impression ... I felt there was a good response … there was recognition that some of the Roman congregations were not helpful in the past. Canon Law is to be updated to take greater account of the problem of clerical child sexual abuse. The obligation to report crimes to the secular state was recognised and will be encouraged.'[8] The sense is of an open, respectful and robust dialogue, and we need to hear more on these lines.

Archbishop Diarmuid Martin has, indeed, gone on record in this vein, noting time and again the deeper roots of our ecclesial crisis in Ireland and occasionally being explicitly critical of dealings with Roman congregations, even if, curiously, seemingly remaining cautious about structural reform.[9]

I note, in addition, the more recent Advent 2010 Pastoral Letter of Bishop Bill Murphy of Kerry in which, reporting on a Diocesan Listening Exercise from May 2010 in response to Pope Benedict's letter to the Irish people, he writes that he is 'committed to the empowerment of lay people based on real collaboration at all levels, and to the inclusion of women in decision-making in our diocese'.[10]

Archbishop Dermot Clifford, chairman of the Bishops' Council for Research and Development, noted, according to reports, that Ireland's 'best, most loyal' Catholics have been 'highly

---

8. Bishop John Kirby at Mass in St Brendan's Cathedral, Loughrea on Sunday 21 February, 2010. Press Release 23 February 2010

9. See homily at 30th anniversary Mass on 20 November 2010 to commemorate Frank Duff, in which Archbishop Martin insists that the abuse scandal has opened our eyes to a much deeper crisis in the Catholic Church in Ireland which has 'lost its way'; and that renewal and reform of the church, in response to this crisis, was 'not about media strategies or structural reform' but would come about from the 'community of men and women who listen to the word of God, who come together to pray, who celebrate the Eucharist and are called to share in the very life of Christ himself' – The Irish Times, Monday, 22 November 2010. It would be strange if Archbishop Martin were to argue against structural reform, not least given his own reform of structures within the Dublin Archdiocese. There is no contradiction between personal and communal conversion on the one hand, and structural reform on the other – on the contrary, the one implies the other, as the church's own teaching on personal and social grace makes clear.

10. Bishop Bill Murphy, Pastoral Letter, Advent 2010

critical' at meetings with bishops and that this was also found to be the case in surveys conducted on behalf of the Catholic Church in Ireland, which, when processed, will have 'a huge amount to tell the priests and bishops (about) what people are thinking on the ground'.[11]

And finally, Bishop Seamus Freeman of Ossory, reporting on the beginnings of a structured dialogue involving lay faithful in response to the papal Letter, notes that the participants expressed disappointment 'that child sexual abuse was not seen as a symptom of shortcomings in church structure and function in the pope's letter', that there 'was no critique of the role of the Vatican, and little or no acknowledgment of the exclusion of lay people from roles in which they can contribute' and that 'many respondents called for dialogue relating to sexuality, clerical celibacy and the exclusion of women (not just from ordination)'.[12]

On a different, but related issue I note that it will also be appropriate to think through the method and criteria used for the appointment of bishops, with much more transparency and wider consultation to be recommended, including the effective involvement of lay faithful. We need, with Rome, to question what has now become the custom of exclusively Roman appointments to the episcopacy.

4. *The Episcopal Conference needs to act more effectively*
The resistance of some bishops to collegiality in Vatican II was not so much to do with relationships with the papacy as with the desire to maintain autonomy within the area of their own Episcopal Conference. The initial incompetent response of the Irish Episcopal Conference to the child sexual abuse scandal has been a great let-down. Of course, since then, thankfully, progress has been made, not least with the establishment of the National Board for Safeguarding Children in the Catholic Church under Ian Elliot. But there is little sense of effective

11. *The Irish Times*, Monday 6 December 2010
12. Bishop Seamus Freeman, Chairman of the Bishops' Council for Pastoral Renewal and Adult Faith Development, op cit.

decision-making and communication from the Episcopal Conference and this is a great scandal – not just because of the CSA issue, but, more widely, because it leaves a significant leadership vacuum in our church. This issue cannot be allowed to drift on with a shrug of the shoulders or on the pretext of a theological appeal to the primacy of the bishop in his own diocese. There is a responsibility on our bishops to act and communicate cohesively and effectively and it is incumbent on them to make the appropriate organisational and cultural changes to allow this to happen.

Following the analysis presented here it seems to me the most effective initiative the Episcopal Conference could take would be to empower lay involvement in the church, according to the vision of Vatican II. I recall the words of Cardinal Tomás Ó Fiaich at the 1987 Synod of Bishops, when he advocated that the hierarchy needed to set about 'awakening the sleeping giant' that is the laity, going on to note that 'feminism can no longer be considered middle-class madness or an American aberration' (Fahey, 334).

I would suggest further that the best way to bring about this empowerment would be to convene a National Assembly of the Irish Church, in preparation for which there would be discussion at all levels – parish, diocese, episcopal conference – and including an outreach to the disaffected and already alienated from the institutional church. The assembly might be focused on some kind of open question like: 'In the Spirit of Jesus Christ, what sort of church do we want for the future?' This project would give cohesion and energy to all the local, diocesan and even national initiatives mentioned in nn 2 and 3 above and would send out a strong signal that the Irish Catholic Church, in repentance and humility, wants to fulfill its divinely mandated mission to our world. There is a danger, unfortunately, given the overly-bureaucratic and ineffective nature of the Episcopal Conference, that bishops will satisfy themselves with having 'listened' to the faithful, with little effective follow-up. The bishops need to grasp the need for 'accountable listening' and a National

Assembly, with appropriate follow-up mechanism built in, would be a clear signal that they had grasped this need and were prepared to exercise real leadership.[13]

5. *Engagement of the Irish Church with Rome*

Again there needs to be a more robust, adult engagement of the whole Irish church with the church of Rome. As I have argued consistently in these pages, I think there are many good reasons for strong central leadership, but not at the expense of local autonomy. The German bishops are representing strongly about the details of a new German translation of the Missal: we are faced with the introduction of a new English version this year, the process towards which was extremely controversial, and yet there seems to have been little public expression of views by the Irish Hierarchy. Why? And what of the publicly stated desire of the bishops a number of years ago to introduce the more communal forms of the Sacrament of Reconciliation on a more regular basis in Ireland: why did they simply acquiesce to Roman demands not to do so? Again, one is not arguing for dissent for its own sake, not even for a re-run of the famous controversy over the date of Easter which saw Ireland and Rome lock horns in the past. What is involved, rather, is a more adult assumption of responsibility for oversight of the Irish church – a God-given mission of the Irish episcopacy.

One does well to anticipate the difficulties of this kind of approach: '…which of you, intending to build a tower, would not first sit down and work out the cost to see if he had enough to complete it? … or again, what king marching to war against another king would not first sit down and consider whether with ten thousand men he could stand up to the other who advanced against him with twenty thousand?' (Lk 14:28-32). Would 'standing up' to Rome mean acrimony in the short-term and simple defeat in the long-term and, if so, can that be a prudent way to proceed? Because, down the road, this more assertive

---

13. See Appendix for fuller account of the rationale and nature of a National Assembly.

way of acting might well involve a questioning of Rome about canon 129 (the role of laity in decision-making), about the proper authority of Episcopal Conferences, about the canonical status of synods, about the other controverted issues touched upon here around ecclesial teaching on sex and gender. But Irish Catholics know well that it is not in the gift of our bishops to solve all outstanding issues, and they would not expect this. What would help, though, is if the Irish bishops alerted Rome to the simple fact that certain teaching has not been received in peace by the Irish church. Of course we are far from this point now, but it is as well to anticipate what may happen if the Irish bishops agree 'to take the lid off' and allow for a more generous space for discussion within the church. If that happens, and if issues arise which Ireland on its own cannot handle, it would still be a wonderful service to the universal church if Ireland was able to request a Third Vatican Council to broach such issues, including, of course, the reform of the Roman Curia that has already been mentioned. This kind of respectful representation has a long and venerable tradition in our church – going back at least to Paul's reprimand of Peter over his attitude to the Gentiles – and, done in the proper spirit, would be both courageous and prudent.

6. We need to recruit the skills of many disciplines in our project

I refer of course to theologians, canon lawyers, historians but also to political scientists, social psychologists, cultural experts, group facilitators and so on – the issue we face is complex, and if liberating the voice of the faithful is a necessary first step it will not be sufficient on its own. It will take skill and expertise, as well as goodwill and boldness, to engender those habits of conversation and decision making within our church in a way that does not destabilize the many other vital forces that are at work in the body of the church, not least the effective leadership from the centre. Again, we need with humility to acknowledge the help we can obtain from secular fields of expertise. I can imagine, for example, that many bishops would be daunted by the proposal to have a National Assembly of the Irish Church since they themselves might not have the skills to facilitate such a meeting and could only imagine a kind of chaos ensuing which would have detrimental effects. But this need not be so – there is plenty of expertise, both within and outside the Irish Catholic Church (not least from other Christian ecclesial bodies) – which would facilitate a positive outcome.

7. To be a ' light to the world' –
The church, as noted in *LG* and *GS*, exists for the kingdom, to be a light for the world. The holiness of its members – love of God, expressed in love of neighbour – means that the world should find in Catholics a source of hope (anchored in a luminous relationship with God, who is there to save us all and who is faithful to this promise) and of affective and effective companionship to all those who suffer. One senses that too often as church we lose sight of the preferential option of Jesus for the poor, so well expressed in Catholic Social Teaching. We are asked to resist the 'might is right' dynamic running through so much human discourse and activity (the survival of the fittest/greed is good). Why, for example, in Ireland, such a Catholic country for so long, are we noted for a social conservatism rather than a bolder application of Catholic Social Teaching? Our conversation about church vision and structures should never be too introverted or narcissistic: it needs always to be at the service of the wider outreach of Jesus Christ to our world. And of course it is precisely in applying Catholic Social Teaching to the church itself (the dignity of all, the implementation of a model of government that values subsidiarity, solidarity) that we may hope to achieve a greater consistency between what the church preaches and what it practises, and hence to offer a more credible witness to our world. This witness is always needed, not least at this time of national and global financial crisis, with attendant human suffering on a grand scale.

Conclusion

I have argued that the Catholic Church in Ireland – and by implication worldwide – is in need of radical renewal. This need
has been exposed by the scandal of clerical child sexual abuse
and its mishandling by church authorities, but the exposure has
revealed a wider and deeper structural and cultural malaise. At
the heart of this malaise has been the failure to appropriate and
implement the vision of church outlined for us at the Second
Vatican Council, the most authoritative modern faith statement
of ecclesiology. I have proposed seven ways forward as a means
to address this most serious situation. One way of combining
these '7 ways' would be to declare 2012-2015, the 50th anniversary of Vatican II, 'the years of the council' (Orsy, 152), when we
recall its memory and expose ourselves to the transforming light
and force of the Spirit. We could do this in tandem with the
preparation for and holding of a National Assembly or Synod of
the Catholic Church in Ireland. We could do so in the sure hope
of offering a providential response to our calling as church to be
a 'light to the world'.

Towards a National Consultation of the Faithful[1]

There is almost universal agreement – 'from the bishops to the last of the faithful' (St Augustine, as quoted in the Second Vatican Council, *Lumen Gentium*, 12) – that the Irish Catholic Church is in crisis. The crisis is due in the first place to the scandal of clerical child sexual abuse and its even more scandalous mishandling by church authorities, as revealed in several reports (Ferns, Ryan, Murphy, Cloyne to come).

However, as Archbishop Diarmuid Martin has stated on many occasions, the abuse issue has opened people's eyes 'to a much deeper crisis' (*Irish Times*, 22 November 2010). This includes, at a personal level, a growing religious indifference and a drift towards a more secularised vision of life. At institutional level it involves, among other things, an increasing impatience and anger with the distribution of power and the non-collegial exercise of governance at all levels within the Catholic Church, a sense that the continuing absence of the voice and perspective of women in decision-making bodies within the church is unconscionable, and that church teaching on sexuality and gender is foreign to the experience of many good people and is received with incredulity.

There is a growing awareness that, despite the many 'nice' and genuinely good people in positions of authority, the Irish Catholic Church has been mired in a culture of clericalism that is secretive, defensive and excessively deferential. This awareness is reflected in the many informal conversations taking place

---

1. Reproduced, with permission of the editor, from O'Hanlon, *The Furrow*, 62, February, 2011, 88-93

among the faithful, not to mention 'outsiders' and indeed among bishops, priests and religious themselves, peppered by phrases like: 'Things will never change'; 'The church is a horrible place for women'; 'They just don't get it'; 'The bishops themselves are the problem'; 'What kind of parallel universe do they live in?'; 'Get real'.

For many the Irish Catholic Church is no longer a 'light to the world', a 'kind of sacrament or sign of intimate union with God' (*LG*, 1), that space of mystery in which love of God and neighbour is nourished and developed so that God's reign of justice and peace becomes more realisable. In this context Archbishop Dermot Clifford, in an interview to mark the 40th anniversary of the Bishops' Council for Research and Development, is reported as saying that Ireland's 'best, most loyal' Catholics have been 'highly critical' at meetings with bishops and that this was borne out by surveys conducted on behalf of the Catholic Church in Ireland (*Irish Times*, 6 December 2010).

For some, the dimensions of this crisis have been a bridge too far and they have effectively opted out. Many others are hanging on by their finger nails. There are some who dispute the gravity of the situation, taking comfort in the notion that it is was always thus and that Jesus will be with his disciples till the end of time (Mt 28:20).

However, there is also evident the kind of active engagement at parish and diocesan level, described by Mary Redmond and Aoife McGrath in this volume of *The Furrow*, often encouraged by many priests and bishops. In this context one notes, as one among many, the listening exercise carried out since May 2010 in the Diocese of Kerry, published in December 2010 with an accompanying letter by Bishop Bill Murphy stating that 'I am committed to the empowerment of lay people based on real collaboration at all levels, and to the inclusion of women in decision-making in our diocese.'[2] And, at a more national level,

---

2. I also note the remarks of Bishop Murphy at the launch of *Share the Good News*, Wednesday 5 January 2011: '… all too often involvement of the laity is seen by clergy and the laity themselves as 'helping Father'. That is not

Bishop Seamus Freeman, Chairman of the Bishops' Council for Pastoral Renewal and Development, has given an interesting account (*Irish Times*, 28 December 2010) of the beginnings of a national 'structured dialogue' in response to Pope Benedict's Letter to Irish Catholics.

I would suggest that it would be a real sign of hope in our situation if we could envisage a National Consultation (Assembly / Synod – the title can be decided later) of the Irish Catholic Church. This would give focus and added impetus to all the formal and informal conversations taking place at parish, diocesan and even national levels. It would be an earnest of our acceptance of the gravity of our situation and of our desire to respond in a collegial manner which honours the indispensable role of the baptised faithful and is consistent with the vision, letter and spirit of the Second Vatican Council of the church as a *communio* of persons at all levels.

A National Consultation

There are many possible ways to go about the process of a National Consultation. I suggest one, in order to stimulate discussion.

One could set up a Working Party of about 8-12 people (lay faithful, a blend of women and men, theologian, canon lawyer, church historian, sociologist, expert facilitator, priest, religious, bishop). They would advise on the form of a national meeting (assembly / synod?), and initiate a first round of effective consultation of the faithful around some sort of open question like: 'In the Spirit of Jesus Christ, what sort of church do we want for the future?'

On the basis of this consultation, and with further expert

what is envisaged in the documents of the Second Vatican Council, in *Christifideles Laici*, the *Code of Canon Law* and other authoritative documents and statements'; and he goes on to quote from Pope Benedict's address at the Pastoral Convention of the Diocese of Rome in May 2009: 'Consecrated and lay people … must no longer be viewed as 'collaborators' of the clergy but truly recognised as 'co-responsible' for the church's being and action, thereby fostering the consolidation of a mature and committed laity.'

help if required, they might draw up short Working Papers on different topics of concern, to include issues of faith, practice and structures, as they arise.

This group would also advise on who should attend the national meeting (one might envisage groups to include bishops, priests, religious, lay faithful, different social classes, the 'ecclesially disaffected', victims and survivors of clerical child sexual abuse, and members of other ecclesial communities), as well as the method of selecting those who would attend (a mixture of election and appointment?). The group might be helped in their task by seeking advice from other churches who have engaged in a similar process – for example, from participants in the Pastoral Congress in Liverpool in 1980, from other Christian ecclesial communities among whom there is a more habitual practice of synodal discussion.

The time-line for the process might be:

2011-2: Announcement of project by Episcopal Conference, appointment of Working Party who begin initial consultation and draw up working papers.

2012-3: First phase – structured conversation at parish level, with help from working papers

2013-4: Second phase – structured conversation at diocesan level

2014-5: Third phase – National Meeting, with built-in follow up process

This time-line coincides with the celebration of the 50th anniversary of Vatican II (1962-5), but could in fact be considerably abbreviated. The process has the capacity to integrate or to run parallel to other initiatives already under way at parish, diocesan and even national level – one thinks, for example, of the Eucharistic Congress in 2012.

Risks and Opportunities
It might seem that this project is a distraction from the need to address the child abuse scandal or, worse, that it was being used in a cynical way by the church to distract attention from same. It

should be clear from the outset that a National Consultation is no substitute for what the church has already committed herself to in terms of child protection, and that this work should of course continue and be reinforced. However, it is not an insult but rather a tribute to survivors and victims of clerical child sexual abuse that the church should now seek to address the deeper cultural factors which undoubtedly contributed to this great scandal, that it should, in repentance, now seek to 'challenge the prevailing culture'. And, conversely, it is questionable whether the church itself should postpone the National Consultation on the grounds that it's better first for the Cloyne Report to come out, until, in short, the abuse issue is fully addressed. All matters of timing are delicate of course and require prudential judgement: but given that there may be other reports after Cloyne, given that it will take at least a generation to address the abuse issue, is it not better to tackle with urgency the underlying culture which has contributed to our poor response to abuse?

The project might be seen in terms of a structural, managerial 'fix' at odds with that 'mystery' of the church of which the Second Vatican Council speaks (*LG*, 1) and which is rooted deeply in faith. However, we know that in the incarnation mystery and the divine took flesh and that culture, structures and institutions are part of God's kingdom and need addressing, just as personal conversion also does. The words of Archbishop Diarmuid Martin are apt: '... renewal and reform of the church ... will only come from within the church, that is from the community of men and women who listen to the Word of God, who come together to pray, who celebrate Eucharist and are called to share in the very life of Christ himself' (homily, 20 November 2010). But, of course, this renewal will be institutional as well as personal – the two go together, as Archbishop Martin has acknowledged in several other contexts.[3] In order to ensure that

---

3. One notes his insistence on the establishment of Parish Councils within the Archdiocese of Dublin, and his call for a 'broad National Forum on the future of educational provision and the place of faith education within the Irish educational system ...' (Address at the launch of *Share the Good News*, Wednesday 5 January 2011).

this faith dimension remains primary throughout the process, it would be important that prayer and worship are intrinsic to every stage – we want to be engaged in a discernment of where the Holy Spirit is leading, which will include but cannot be reduced to factors of organisation and management.

It might be feared that this project could be infected by a Pelagian, even Pharasaical zeal for perfection that failed to realise the eschatological truth that the church in its pilgrim way is gifted with a 'holiness that is genuine though imperfect' (*LG*, 48). We will do well, then, to remember that we are a 'holy church of sinners', without ever using this recognition as a pretext to avoid repenting of our sins.

In this context we will do well also to avoid seeing the initiative in the simplistic terms of a Trojan horse used by 'progressives' to discomfit 'traditionalists'. It would be naïve to suggest that the catholicity of our church does not include the kind of diversity which on some issues extends to outright difference and opposition. We should not use prayer as a way of avoiding these issues, but rather as a way of creating a safe and free space whereby we can learn to respectfully talk and listen to one another, to 'fight fairly' and together find a way forward. Similarly, as in all human endeavours, we can expect new power plays and infighting as the old certainties are questioned. We do not start from scratch in this – our church was founded at a time when its treatment of the Gentiles was the kind of major controversy which threatened unity. This controversy was faced head-on (see, for example, the reprimand of Peter by Paul in Gal 2:13), with confidence in the guidance of the Holy Spirit. We on this island have a secular paradigm of some success in this dialogue involving diversity – the Northern Ireland peace process – from which we can learn. It would seem likely in this context that any National Consultation would be a first rather than a last step in a process – deep differences require time to iron out. In this context one is reminded of the observations of some who took part in the Liverpool Congress in 1980 that while the event itself was successful, there was a failure to follow-up; and of Nuala

O'Loan's proposal that national synods could be held every three years or so (*Studies*, 99, Autumn, 2010, 271).

It might, finally, be objected that bishops could not possibly hope to deliver what might emerge in an open process of accountable listening like this and, if they failed to do so, their last state would be even worse than their first (Lk 11:26). But – as seen by what is already happening in Kerry, Armagh, Down and Connor, Dublin and many, many other dioceses in Ireland – much can and is, gradually, being delivered. It is true that there will inevitably emerge issues which involve the whole church, and Rome in particular, which Irish bishops on their own cannot solve. But Irish Catholics know this well. What would help would be real, accountable listening, an appropriate creative response within Ireland to the issues that can be tackled locally, and then firm representation to the wider church, including Rome, with respect to those issues of current church teaching and/or law which are not being 'received' within Ireland in peace. This might even, in time, lead to the convocation of a Third Vatican Council to address the serious outstanding issues that face the universal church, in which case the Irish church would have done the whole church some service.

The role of bishop in the Ireland of today cannot be an easy one. The temptation to either lie low and hope to ride out the storm, or to exercise 'strong leadership' without accountable listening to the People of God, must be considerable. But the words of the late Cardinal Ó Fiaich at the 1987 Synod of Bishops offer better counsel, when he advocated that the hierarchy needed to set about 'awakening the sleeping giant' that is the laity, going on to note that 'feminism can no longer be considered middle-class madness or an American aberration'.[4] To give space to the lay faithful to exercise their baptismal responsibilities, even at the expense of some short-term confusion and a stepping back in terms of their own power and control – would

4. Michael A. Fahey, 'Church', in Francis Schüssler Fiorenza, John P. Galvin, eds, *Systematic Theology*, Dublin: Gill and Macmillan, 1992, 327-398, at 334

this not be a worthy contemporary manifestation by bishops of the kind of biblical leadership of service taught by Jesus and exemplified by his washing of feet?

It would of course be possible to envisage some kind of National Consultation of the Irish Catholic Church without episcopal initiation, organised by lay faithful and/or priests, religious. However, it would surely be better for all concerned if the bishops were involved from the start.

Conclusion

With God's help, and in a spirit of repentance and humility, we can use our hearts, minds and imagination to renew our church so that it may, once again, become a 'light for the world'. An effective National Consultation, building on what is happening at parish and diocesan level, would be a major step towards the 'committed programme of ecclesial and individual' renewal called for in the Letter of Pope Benedict XVI (2010, n 2) and so deeply longed for by Irish Catholics.

Callaghan, Brendan, 'On Scandal and scandals: the psychology of clerical paedophilia', *Studies*, 99, Autumn, 2010, 267-275

Clifford, Archbishop Dermot, Report of interview in *The Irish Times*, Monday, 6 December 2010

Corkery, James and Worcester, Thomas, eds, *The Papacy since 1500*, Cambridge University Press, 2010

Dowling, Bishop Kevin, 'The Current State of the Church', *The Furrow*, 61, November 2010, 591-597

Duffy, Eamon, *Faith of Our Fathers*, London/New York: Continuum, 2004

Dulles, Avery, 'Authority and Conscience', *Church*, Fall, 1986, 8-15

Fahey, Michael A., 'Church', in Francis Schüssler Fiorenza and John P. Galvin, eds, *Systematic Theology, Roman Catholic Perspectives*, Dublin: Gill and Macmillan, 1992, 327-398

Freeman, Bishop Seamus, 'Rite and Reason', *The Irish Times*, Tuesday, 28 December 2010

Gallagher, Michael Paul, *Faith Maps*, London: Darton, Longman and Todd, 2010

Grace, Edmund, 'Democracy, Catholicism and the voice of "faction",' *Studies*, 99, Autumn, 2010, 323-332

Hogan, Linda, 'Mixed reception: Paul VI and John Paul II on sex and war', in Corkery and Worcester, eds, op cit, 204-222

Keenan, Marie, 'An Organizational Cultural Perspective on Child Sexual Abuse in the Catholic Church', *Doctrine and Life*, 60, October, 4-14

Kelly, Kevin T., 'The Pope in Britain', *The Furrow*, 61, 2010, 609-612

Kirby, Bishop John, Homily at Mass in St Brendan's Cathedral, Loughrea on Sunday, 21 February 2010

Lash, Nicholas, *Theology for Pilgrims*, London: Darton, Longman and Todd, 2008

Leahy, Brendan, People, 'Synod and Upper Room: Vatican II's Ecclesiology of Communion', in Dermot A. Lane and Brendan Leahy, eds, *Vatican II, Facing the 21st Century*, Dublin: Veritas, 2006, 49-80

Lennan, Richard, 'Ecclesiology and Ecumenism', in Declan Marmion and Mary E. Hines, eds, *The Cambridge Companion to Karl Rahner*, Cambridge University Press, 2005, 128-143

Lonergan, Bernard J. F., *Method in Theology*, London: Darton, Longman and Todd, 1973 (original 1971)

Mansfield, Dermot, *Heart Speaks to Heart, The Story of Blessed John Henry Newman*, Dublin: Veritas, 2010

Martin, Archbishop Diarmuid, Homily Notes at 30th Anniversary Mass to commemorate Frank Duff, Pro-Cathedral, Dublin, 20 November, 2010, and report in *The Irish Times*, Monday, 22 November 2010

McBrien, Richard P., *The Church*, New York: HarperCollins, 2009 (original 2008)

Murphy, Bishop Bill, *Together in Hope*, Advent Pastoral Letter, 2010

O'Donnell, Christopher, *Ecclesia. A Theological Encyclopedia of the Church*, MN: Liturgical Press, 1996

O'Hanlon, Gerry, 'The Murphy Report – A Response', *The Furrow*, 61, February 2010, 82-91

__ 'The future of the Catholic Church – A view from Ireland', *Studies*, 99, Autumn, 2010, 289-301

— 'Culture and the Crisis in the Church', *The Furrow*, 61, December 2010, 655-666

— 'Towards a National Consultation of the Faithful', *The Furrow*, 62, February 2011, 88-93

O'Loan, Nuala, 'Transparency, accountability and the exercise of power in the Church of the future', *Studies*, 99, Autumn, 2010, 267-275

O'Malley, John W., *What Happened at Vatican II*, Harvard University Press, 2008

Orsy, Ladislas, *Receiving the Council*, MN: Liturgical Press, 2009

Rahner, Karl, 'Structural Change in the Church of the Future', *Theological Investigations*, vol 20, London: Darton, Longman and Todd, 1981, 115-132 (original 1972)

— *The Dynamic Element in the Church*, London: Burns and Oates, 1964

Redmond, Mary, 'Omega: the People's Voice – Reflections on Parish Consultation', *The Furrow*, 62, February 2011, 73-78

Ruth, Sean, 'Responding to Abuse: Culture, Leadership and Change', in Littleton, John and Maher, Eamon, eds, *The Dublin/Murphy Report: A Watershed in Irish Catholicism?*, Dublin: Columba, 2010, 102-112

Shortt, Rupert, *Rowan's Rule*, London: Hodder and Stoughton, 2008

Smith, Bishop Michael, 'An Eyewitness Account', in Lane and Leahy, eds, *Vatican II, Facing the 21st Century*, Dublin: Veritas, 2006, 13-30

Sullivan, Francis A., *Magisterium. Teaching Authority in the Catholic Church*, Dublin: Gill and Macmillan, 1983

— *Creative Fidelity. Weighing and Interpreting Documents of the Magisterium*, Dublin: Gill and Macmillan, 1996

Weakland, Rembert G., *A Pilgrim in a Pilgrim Church*, Michigan/ Cambridge, UK: William B. Eerdmans, 2009

Williams, Rowan, 'Christian unity – theology, practical implications and ecumenical challenges', *The Tablet Speeches*, 13 December, 2010